# FLOORED!

Maiche Lev

If they called me
"Jaw, I'd buy
A VIOLA & retire.

— ML —

# FLOORED!

by Maiche Lev
All Rights Reserved
Copyright © 2018 HDW Publications

Cover and book design by David Bricker

ISBN:978-0-9975757-2-9

http://www.maichelev.com

# Set List

Dedication ........................................... i

Epigraph ........................................... iii

The Music I'm Listenin' To ........................... 1

Waffle House Scuddles ............................... 7

Johnny Hates Jazz ................................... 11

Catcher's Mitt Plagiarist ............................. 19

Hey Rockstar ....................................... 21

My House ........................................... 23

And I'm a Doo-Dah Man .............................. 27

Griggsby Girl! ...................................... 31

Late January Morning Song ........................... 35

David Goodman's Song ............................... 41

Kings of Kool ....................................... 63

Swimming Tips ...................................... 71

Break on Through ................................... 75

Rocky Balboa's Mom's Salon on 71st Street ........... 79

Harvey Weinstein (No Relation) ...................... 89

Fuck ............................................... 91

I Danced and Sang ................................... 95

New and Newsworthy ................................ 101

Full Half-a-Zappa Freak ............................. 105

It's Rainin' in New Orleans .......................... 107

Ha' t' Git Down in Dat Water ........................ 111

Detroit Leslie ...................................... 113

Than Listen to This 80's Crap, I'd Rather… ......117

Featherweight in Pounderville............................119

Prince Rogers Nelson ....................................125

I Need to Thank the Lord ...............................127

Mahalia ....................................................129

Become a Singer ........................................133

Rubbed y' Wrong...........................................141

My Old Friend Ralph .....................................145

Virgil, Quick Come See (Splashdown) ..............153

What do I want for my Birthday? .....................155

To Those Few Brave Men at

    Resurrection Drums: .................................159

Go Mickey! ................................................167

Oh No, Oh No ............................................169

Punk.........................................................171

Some of Tom Petty's Other Greatest Hits..........173

Shira A .....................................................175

Doin' Sound is Doin' Sound

    (for a peaceful warrior) ............................179

It's Like ....................................................195

Saying Vespa...............................................199

How Does It Feel?........................................201

Song for Lisa Mimosa ...................................209

Japanese ...................................................213

Dave's Song................................................217

Laundries, Bars, Hamburgers, Bookstores .......225

Titty Time Bar Song..........................................237

House of the Rising Sun (Alternate lyrics) ........241

Laugh a Little ...............................................  243

Rags.............................................................249

Kid Gone Bad ..................................................253

Maybe French? ...............................................257

These Children...............................................263

Last December Late.........................................267

Pictures of Petty ...........................................269

Author's Note.................................................271

Endnotes.......................................................273

# FLOORED!

# DEDICATION

Raise your voice in song
And make a sweet sound

For a secret hero, Howie Epstein
God, he could sing!
And there were a lot of tears

With great respect for
Mike Campbell
Benmont Tench
Ron Blaire
Stan Lynch
Steve Ferrone
Scott Thurston
And Tom Petty

And John Prine
Del Shannon
Bobby Dylan
And all those who knew Howie and loved him
His family and friends

He's a part of what we hear…
What we *love* to hear

Thank you, Howie Epstein
Thank you for being so good
May one such as you my escort one day be

Raise your voice in song
And make a sweet sound

# Epigraph

From the stage they'll be trying to get water out
of rocks

—Bob Dylan

The bad nights take forever
And the good nights never seem to last

—Tom Petty

We're gonna be up here tonight till we feel like we've
really played.

—T.P

We touched the ground at JFK
Tonight this city belongs to me

—"Angel of Harlem," U2

We're the band that found the distance to the stage
too far

—Pete Townsend

I'd like to thank the New York City Police
Department and everyone in the crowd selling
loose joints

—Paul Simon

Hello to all you at home
I hope you're getting loose
Drinking a few beers
Smoking a few joints

—Mick Jagger

People stay ... Just a little bit longer
—The Zodiacs (peformed by Jackson Browne)


Living on a lighted stage approaches the unreal
—Geddy Lee


We're runnin' a little hot tonight.

—Van Halen


This is what I do
This is what I's made to do
We're here for you night after night after night
   after night

—Bruce Springsteen


Here I am on the road again
There I am up on the stage
There I go playing star again
There I go...

—Bob Seger

# THE MUSIC I'M LISTENIN' TO

You look like the music I'm listenin' to
Aw, look at you
If you're not 58, you're 62
Fishin' for a cigarette
Smilin'
Gap-toothed
Nothin' special 'bout today
Parking lot, asphalt, late afternoon
Yes you do, mama
You look like the music I'm listenin' to

Don't you look like the music I'm listenin' to?
Aw, look at you
Surfer boys and surfer girls
*Shangri-la-la-loo*
Someone brought a tambourine
A beat-up guitar
A radio, too
Nothin' special 'bout today
Tide's low
Be high by noon
Play me something — play me a tune
You look like the music I'm listenin' to

You look like the music I'm listenin' to
Aw, look at you
You're such a heartbreaker
Your little friend there's a heartbreaker, too
There's a DJ inside
Saturday night
Lively crew
Nothing special 'bout today
They know all the words just like we used to
You look like the music I'm listenin' to

You look like the music I'm listenin' to
It's a band from San Francisco, California
They were formed in the year of '49
It's not hard to understand how they got *way*
    too good
People 'd come and wait in line
People 'd come and travel with the band
Girls and guys
College kids
Mountain folk
Country blues with some kinda funk
Sure, I'll take a toke
To hear it was to love it, man
It fills your heart, stirs your head

You look like the music I'm listenin' to
A 'band beyond description,' The Grateful Dead

*Whoop-dee-doo*
You look like the music I'm listenin' to
Aw, look at you
*Wopp-ah-pa-loo-bop-a-wap-bam-boom...*[1]
What a little volume can do!
Nothing special 'bout today
'cept a chance to get carried away
God only knows what I'd be without you[2]
Yes, you look like the music I'm listenin' to

You look like the music I'm listenin' to
I've had enough talk radio for a lifetime or two
When it's too early for rock 'n' roll ...
It's still too early for *you*
Nothing special 'bout today
The Baltimore Ravens came out psyched on U2
"Where the Streets Have No Name"
And they'd won the game
When the final whistle blew
You look like the music I'm listenin' to

You look like the music I'm listenin' to
Bob Marley and Peter Tosh, the Bunny Wailer crew
When they weren't rehearsing, it was the BBC they
   were listenin' to
The Clash pulled up in a cab rollin' up a cigar-
   sized doob
Nothin' special 'bout t'day
What the rich may squander
What the poor can't afford to do
You look like the music I'm listenin' to

You look like the music I'm listenin' to
Washington Square Park
What else is there to do?
Madison Square Garden
That was me gettin' crazy next to you
A half a belly full of wine
Pass around a little vine
Have you ever tried the British Columbian kind?
*Pheww!*
You look like the music I'm listenin' to

You look like the music I'm listenin' to
Some people never get carried away
Never spend a stoned day

Might've been me
If I'd a never heard the stuff my friends had
  me play
There'd be nothin' special 'bout t'day
*Sketches of Spain*
Feelin' *Kind of Blue*
Half-drunk on *Bitch's Brew*
You look like the music I'm listenin' to

You look like the music I'm listenin' to
Ladysmith Black Mambazo
"Diamonds on the Souls of Her Shoes"
The Indestructible Beat of Soweto
A violin in the ghetto
Little Richard
Lionel Hampton
Robert Johnson got somethin' to show you
You look like the music I'm listenin' to

Yes, you look like the music I'm listenin' to
You look like the music I'm listenin' to

# WAFFLE HOUSE SCUDDLES

Do I spend more on these jukebox numbers
Than I do on these scrambled eggs?
At this hour of the night
Whole town's in bed

I spend more on this jukebox
Than I do on a bran muffin with raisins
The whole place sings along with Garth
"I Got Friends in Low Places"

Oh, to put ten dollars in the thing
And slink down with paper and pen
Hash browns and grits
"Black tonight, Bonnie, and please keep it comin'…
I'm here with the hits"

Starin' out the window
I know I'm in chains
The kind of chains nobody sees[3]
And I don't want to know ya
And I don't want to see ya
Lord God, don't I need Seals and Crofts'
   "Summer Breeze?"

I put more in this box than I spend on my coffee
"I Can Feel it Comin' in the Air Tonight"
"Hold on"
Table 6 needs a rag
Bring a mop for table 3
They *lose* it over Phil Collins' tom-toms

Don't I put more in this Jukebox
Than I do in the register, Louise?
Could you have the cook
Warm these up once more for me please

If I'm not here past three
I'm 'cross town at *that* greasy spoon
"Tuesday's Gone"
"Delta Dawn"
Marvin's singin', "What's going on?"
Greasy spoons
Hard-boiled eggs and stewed prunes

Play it again one more time, Joe
"It's survival in the City
When you're livin' day to day
City streets don't have much pity
When you're down that's where you'll stay"⁴
Oh… *(guitars!)*

I like to come here to get some work done
Dawn, she breaks
"Here Comes the Sun"
Heck I got my own radio station!
Late night
A hypothetical destination
"Sweet Baby James" in the rotation

The Waffle House
Well lit
Clean and comfortable
Warm in winter
Always friendly and affordable
Liver and onions to die for
Hope to be back around sometime real soon
Play y'all some more good rockin' tunes

# Johnny Hates Jazz
## (with Dave Bricker)

Johnny hates jazz
He don't know, but he do
Johnny hates jazz
Jazz he don't do
Jazz is well-dressed people eating hors d'oeuvres
You always hear "Summertime" or "My
    Favorite Things"
It gets on your nerves

Johnny hates jazz
Jazz is tame
Only mildly insane
Jazz…

You could say Oscar Peterson
Was the tracks beneath the train

Jazz…
What is it?
*Jazz…?*
*Come on …*
*Step it out, baby*
*Jive*

*Old school*
*C'mon … step*
*Hear that snare?*
*Tap it out*
*Hit it!*

Blackened windows on 59th Street
Heroin chic
Jazz is *shuffle*
The color blue
Jazz paints itself a picture
In the time it takes to
Jazz has its own voodoo

Jazz
They play it in New Orleans
And in Utah…
Or at least I heard they do
*Sketches of Spain*
In those changing times
*Sketches of Spain*
Before he was angry all the time

Jazz…
A man in every corner
Giving all he's got

Man, they built it up
Those guys played *good*
Those guys played *hot*

Jazz piano…
Is *ice*
Jazz piano
Play that number again
Never played the same way twice

Jazz piano is the rod
Jazz piano is the hammer
The tones
The chime
The bells
The nails
The bones

Jazz
I once heard someone play jazz music
On a banjo
Whodathunkit?
A *banjo!*
"The Cosmic Hippo"
"The Sinister Minister" brings it on home

Jazz
Who might have coined the name?
"Jazz…"
Probably just somebody
Sittin' on a curb
Listenin' to some folks makin' it last
*Yeah … Jazz …jazzy … a jazz fest*

*I think my cats like jazz, man*
*Whenever that latenight program is on*
*They turn over on their backs*
*Crazy paws*
*Eyes wide open*

*No…*

*Yeah*

*11:00 PM*
*FM 93.1*
*It's like nip to them or somethin'*

Jazz
Buddy Rich will *bust you up*
Jazz is vodka
Champagne

A line of cocaine
Nobody tells old Freddie Green to hurry it up
Johnny
You really can't hate jazz
It's a prelude to a dance
A lot of people are touched
By its poetry
Its elegance

Johnny
Miami got jazz
The beloved China Valles
Smooth Len Paice
The real Tracy Fields
Fillin' in that after-midnight space

Jazz
Baby…
Be-bop, scree-bop, dooby-doo
Frisco
Miami
New York
Chicago
The chicken cordon bleu…
The Portobello mushroom
The Cobb salad

Clams casino
Chocolate fondue
Unforgettable
There'll never be another you
Yardbird? Sweet!
So what?
Smoke gets in your eyes
It's only a paper moon
We're struttin' with some barbecue

I got rhythm
I got music
I got my gal
Who could ask for anything more?[5]
If be-bop gave way to swing
Jazz made 'em dance and sing
Bewitched, bothered, and bewildered

You can't hate jazz, Johnny
It come from the street
A backbeat
Swing
Ride
Brushes
Bass

Keys
Strings
*Listen…*

*Listen … It's* Canteloupe Island

*C'mon…!*

*Jazz … it's a scream*
*Jazz … it's a hoot*
*Johnny, c'mon*
*The band ain't through!*

# CATCHER'S MITT PLAGIARIST

Yeah, 'Catcher's Mitt Plagiarist' for a working title...
I speak this shade of the language
You can have the rest
David Fricke with *Rolling Stone*
He could babble for a week
Rock and roll is what he speaks
He can prove it's an artform
The strangest religion ever born
"Out on Thunder Island"

*Doo-doo-doo-doo*
*Doo-doo-doo*
*Doo-doo-doo*
*Doo-doo-doo-doo-dooh*
*Yeah, yeah, yeah...*

# HEY ROCKSTAR

Amy, you broke hearts
You never knew you could do such a thing
The face on you
A candle in the wind
Little wing
Into the great wide open
Hurrying home after school
To close the door and sing
They laid flowers in the rain
All around Hyde Park
You were going to help us
With this box of broken parts
Amy, you broke hearts
I can still see your face
You played the tart
We'll see you in the stars
When the music starts
Amy

# MY HOUSE

My house smells like a veterinarian's office
Now that the windows are all closed in
The police come by three times 'bout the noise
  at night
So now its dogs and incense
A cigarette den
And I don't even want to talk about the flea situation
Go ahead
Sit wherever you choose
It's borderline infestation

And these roaches
Where do they come from?
A line of ants dancin' in the kitchen
Inspecting my Fig Newtons
There's sand in the bathtub
Slow drain
Water gathers
The film is enough to turn you away
You could skim a bar of soap
*Yuck!*
One that really lathers

I've got a cat in all this mess
She and I don't share much love
I can't get used to how she prowls at my legs
I must confess to a toss or a shove
I lost my backpack just last week
Address book, and checks, too
But my wallet was in my back pocket
I got it! Yippie! Yahoo!

It's been a windy day today
Sky's clouded east to west
I've got things to do, but one of my dogs has run off
So I'm sitting here writing this jest
It's the second of the month
Tomorrow the third
I'll turn thirty-something years old
I kinda wish my ex-wife
Would come by and lay somethin' on me
Somethin' wild
Somethin' bold

Oh, I'm sittin' right here
In the center of town
Seems a place forever I've been
I'm sittin' out here on the highway side

Summertime
Wisconsin


It's like a second hand store in the city
Or a fruit stand in the plains
It's like a thousand telephones that don't ring[6]
Or a stamp collection that reigns

# AND I'M A DOO-DAH MAN

I play more in a month's time now, than I ever did as
  a kid
My time is all bottled up, and I'm shaken
The tap is to the lid
And I'm aiming for my personal best
And I know when I feel good
Or content or appeased or satisfied
Knowing that I've done near all I could
And I'm a Doo-Dah man

Big verbal announcement:
"I play the drums!"
An announcement of sorts
I'm looking for a rock-n-roll rhythm-and-blues,
   country outfit
That really rips-n-snorts
Hoots and Hollers, lulls-n-cries
And packs it up to go
Nashville, Six Street, Muscle Shoals
Now get me to the show!
Goddamn!
I'm a Doo-Dah man.

Mr. Levon Helm
How he could play and sing
And that was The Band
Don Henley—he could pull it off, too
And that cat from the Romantics, man
You understand
We could do some time
Lose some sleep
Come off smooth
As loose as tweaked
Saddle up that drum
Tell everyone
To get it right
This Saturday night
*Bam!*
I'm a Doo-Dah man

Beginners
Advanced beginners
Amateurs
Pros
Everyday there's a step to be built
A riser to be stood on, don't ya know
And it's real
Sure as twenty-four hours makes a day

And I'm standin' right here
I'll take my rest when I take my rest
Thelonious Monk's middle name was "Sphere"
Play it again, Sam!
"T" was a Doo-Dah man

I look forward to meeting you, whoever you are
So we can share some times
I've got my own stepstools
My own set of tools
You won't feel me on your back as we climb
The ground's been cleared in my back yard
A foundation's been poured
A satellite dish for makin' a wish
A laser beam from the *ward*
I'm a Doo-Dah man

Yeah, I used to be some kind of folk singer
I must 've written a hundred songs
But I forgot 'em all
And I bought some drums
And now I just sing along
Those few songs I'd like to remember that I've lost
That were a part of me…
Well, they were cast to the wind

On a river of gold
That flows into an auburn sea
And I'm a Doo-Dah man

I play more in a month's time now than I ever did
   as a kid
My time is all bottled-up and I'm shaken
The tap is to the lid
Aiming for my personal best
I know when I feel good
Or content or appeased or satisfied
Knowing I've done near all I could

Don't that make me a Doo-Dah man?

# GRIGGSBY GIRL!

I am Channing Griggs
Start to finish

I am a sun-drenched apricot colored fourth year
   deckhand-pirate-mermaid
Playing a muscular Cuban flute
On a too small, vintage, somewhat rickety, black-
   hulled, wooden sailing craft
On the archipelago Caribbean

I am a child of ten being told to "please sit up"
As I sternly practice and practice
And practice and practice…
My long
Black
Heavy clarinet

I am in Albany, New York, picking apples

I am doing my laundry

I am walking Rhoda, my Rhodesian Ridgeback

I am in Miami with the boys
Laying down sax solos in the style of Bobby Keys
Of The Rolling Stones fame

I am feeling pretty good at yet another airport
Renting yet another car
To take myself to yet another festival
Where yet another group of musicians
Are celebrating yet another day of living

Oh Boy!
I am tasting apple schnapps for the first time
Playing in a Yiddishkeit Klesmer outfit …
Nutty!

I am ten years a senior
To the young beauty-rebel music student in front
    of me
With her dreadnought acoustic guitar
Her eggroll
And her mug of ginger-ale

I am strumming a banjo
Working on "Smile"
The third song I've learned

From a new collection just released by Alan and
  Neil Lomax

I am thirty-two years of age

I don't speak French but I think I can…
And that works

I am sitting on a coffee table
Laughing hard at myself on video
In a way-off-Broadway production
Of Woody Guthrie's *House of Earth*
I got to play Ellie May, his very pregnant wife
(Y' need something to do in Albany other than
  pick apples)

I am busking in my beloved French Quarter

I am reading by campfire light

I am going to the movies with my boyfriend's kid

I am absolutely loving some stinky cheese on
  a baguette

I am listening to a live Bob Marley album,
   *Babylon by Bus*
(Aren't you just glad sometimes that reggae
   music happened?)

I am *so* ready to formalize
All the collected informal momentum of
   my talents
(Yes, a degree)

I am a student
My former 2.6 GPA has been elevated to 3.7
The Dean's List at Broward College

I am Channing Griggs
Crossing your campus

I am Channing Griggs
Start to finish

# LATE JANUARY MORNING SONG

Yes
I guess
I'll be the captain and you'll be Tennille
And we'll take over F.M. radio

I've got it!
It'll rocket!
A cheeky little number
And away we go!

Never mind the apartment
Never mind the rent
We're gonna sing this song in forty different
countries
Before the sun is set

Just got off the phone with Frank and Bob
They're on their way over
They heard the opening lick
And quit their day jobs

And Linda Ringer
The background singer

She heard the riff and nearly wet her pants
She got so excited
She could barely hide it
We're talkin'
*Big*
  *Record company*
    *Advance*

Dude, listen…
It's catchy
Gets your attention
Right here, little needle scratchy
Into the horns of the Fifth Dimension

Pretty hip, no?
The hell if it ain't original
Get this…
It came to me while I was sleeping
How can we lose?
It's country blues
Add some clave and bongos
We'll go Puerto Rican

We'll record it
They'll adore it
Maybe L.A.

Wimbley
Sidney
New York
All the way

It's unique!
*Magnifique!*
A Top-40 international hit
(Yeah) Freak!
Top of the charts in a couple of months
If not a couple of weeks!

Oh, Yes
God Bless
She'll be peaches
I'll be cream
Barry White
Dynamite
The Hollywood Bowl screamin' dream

We'll play "Clear to the Moon"
"Memphis in June"
We'll play "That's the Way I Like It"
We re-do the Beatles' "Yesterday"
And Ray Charles' "What I Say"
And when they can't get enough…

The ticket price, we'll hike it!
Easy listening
Bridge
Harmonics
Nice
Irresistible ear candy
Gibson splice

A great pop song
Can't run too long
Love is lost
Love is won

We can use violins
From Franks MIDI-systems
Call and response
It's a sing-along
Sing it. Sing it. Sing it. Sing it
Sing a Song
Sing a Song!

She's so somethin'
She's my dumpling
What's it gonna say?
He's so lonely,
For his one and only

It's all a big joke, anyway
Celebration
Jubilee
Concert Hall
Tour bus number 1
Tour bus number 2
Tour bus number 3

Yes
I guess
I'll be The Captain and you'll be Tennille
And we'll take over FM radio
So, it's lights down!
Turn it up!

*And away we go…*

# DAVID GOODMAN'S SONG

We all loved David Goodman
He was pretty like Alanis Morrisette
Like Jackson Browne
Crewneck sweater, oxford shirt
Full-lipped, blue-eyed
Catalogue material—L.L. Bean in a red vest of down
With that New England accent
Incredulously walking around
With a laugh none of his buddies could live down
*Hey, Davie!*

Those mornings in Maine
The dew on the grass would seep through
    your high-tops
Cold milk
Hot cocoa in pitchers
Greasy eggs over easy
I believe the cook's name was N'korschukke
Yeah, Good ol' sweaty Jim N'korschukke

*Hmmm*
The full picture windows in the mess hall
Were held up with metal clasps

The bathroom doors swung
With creaking hasps
Rough hewn, untreated hardwood everywhere
A rec hall as big as a barn
Down yonder there

Minor league baseball
Wooden backstops painted brown
A grand ski dock
Two-dozen plank picnic tables, mid campus
We even had a bike shop
With ten-speeds in good shape
For rides into Casco town

Do you remember those hotdog buns?
Could've been made of sourdough bread
Not your average crusty hotdog buns…
More like challah bread
We were well fed
*Later, we'll get to the steak'ums*

Alright…
The Bible according to *Penthouse's* Bob Guccione
It left us tired
Feckless, but laughing
It was innocent enough, I guess

Bunks full of boys up past dark
Bedsprings and backboards a-rapping and a-tapping

We had our own lockers each year
Our bunks had porches and screen doors
Every bunk maroon
Every blade of grass green
Maine
Across the lake there'd come sudden squalls
Winds within winds
The sky 'd turn black
Dark storms
"Get back to your bunks!"
Counselors' calls

What year was it?
I can't say
No one could decide
Whether the "The Devil Went Down to Georgia"
Or "Alabama Getaway" was their favorite song
Then there was Bad Company's " Rock and
    Roll Fantasy"
"Fire in the sky; tearin' up the ground"

The big kids:
There was "Peanut" with his asthma

Mark Vie with his quarterback dreams
*God, he could throw!*
Robbie Wolfson with his orange and yellow E.P.
   slalom skis
And "E.D.", Eric Daniels
Now there was a kid who could who could
   do *anything*
A secret hero
And the Schnur brothers
David beat me on the tennis court during
   color wars


Now my best friends at camp
Were Scotty Davis and Sammy Seder
Scott was a fine baseball player
And he had all of his sister's Dylan records on the
   cassette player
But really, Scott was a basketball ace and a south-
   paw at that
A real deadringer
And listen, if we had a girl's camp come in for
   a social, a dance
Scott became *Earth, Wind & Fire's* Commodore
   lead singer
He could ham it up, man!

Pure exuberance
*All my love, Scotty*


And what about Sammy Seder?
Well, I hear that since way back then he's been
  to college
Pre-law, but he done cursed that profession
Then, I hear he went out to Hollywood
Copped a part in a sitcom that ran one summer
That's a tough sell, summer television
(The cat looks just like Neil Sedaka, I failed
  to mention)
So after reading *The Atlantic Review*
And having done near half of *all* there is to do
Sam can be heard on the moaning, groaning
  AM radio stations
Hey Sam, Congratulations!
*Lord of the Flies*
(Encore, fat bags)


The original sleep apnea patient on this earth
His name was Weiner — Scott Weiner
How did he ever end up sleeping next to me that
  last summer
In senior boys?

His snoring would wake you
Just as you were driftin' off
He would *quake* you deep in the night
He'd suck deep and shake the cabin's rafters
Before reveille's noise

We had this baseball coach named Brian Bowers
One summer during a home game tournament
I strangely remember him packing the entire third
    base line
With wheelbarrows full of what seemed to be red
    clay putty
Matty on third
Levine pitched some
Sadowski caught (Sau!)
Herschberg, Andy
Brian's teams were crackerjack
Having been sun-drilled
"Adler!"
"Schnur!"
"Sher!"
"Kaplan!"
"Peretz!"
"Leider!"
"Blum"!
"Davis!"

"Seder!"
"Look alive out there!"
"Here we go now!"


There were biddy basketball courts
'Neath the high and mighty old pines
Lining the winter-shredded back road
The red clay tennis courts
Were like those of the French Open
Extra soft and super slow


Come June in Maine
Just a month after May's arrival
After April's stubborn thaw
Sebago Lake's tributaries were still quite, quite cold
And us Miami boys were not used to such a plunge
No one was
Shivers
Quivers
Lord, I'm talkin' *cold*
Yeah, second day in camp
You had to take this "twenty minute swim"
If you wanted to use the drink
You had to do it if you wanted to sail a sunfish
Ski behind the orange *Baja* or *The Tique*
Kayak or fish

(DIP…, dip… dip, dip, dip, dip)
(DIP…, dip… dip, dip, dip, dip)
If you could get an older counselor
Or a counselor in training (a CIT)
To stop off at Mario's Pizza or McDonalds
And wake you up just past midnight…
Well that was huge
*Huge!*

When you're ten or eleven years old
Packages from home are the *shit*—I mean the
    goods
It was embarrassing
I almost always got one
*Thanks, Mom*

We could be cruel to kids
Who were a little bit quirky or peculiar
We taunted them
There were a few each year
Sad-eyed Danny, Adam, George, Kent
We were cruel
It was a shame
Real hurt
Like *condemned*

I mean, imagine a young soul stuck in a bunk
With a bunch of snots like us
Pickin' and pickin' and pickin' on you
It would be eight whole weeks
Of wishin' you were somewhere else
Eight weeks of cryin' in the office
Calling home
Bitter fruit
We were warned to stop
*Or else…*


How in the world did our bunk
Get to watch the all-star game that year?
We were on the floor in the director's house
Bunk 13 was so bad one year
There was fire
Broken glass
Kids were sent home
Dave Gutman was a force
A midfielder
Maryland lacrosse


Should I tell you about the canoe trip
When we took a wrong route
And damn near found out

What it'd be like to cascade over a nasty bit of rock?
And that awful summer
When we learned that drinking and driving
   don't mix?
Two beautiful young men in a car
And that tree by the side of the road
Its trunk all scarred
We passed by in silence
Scott Harris
David Berkowitz

On a brighter note
Once a week on Sundays
The whole camp would pile into full-sized yellow
   school buses
And take to travelin'
To places with names like Old Orchard Beach
Ogunquit
The Piscataqua Bridge
We loved it!

And then on rainy days
Somehow we'd all end up rollerskating
A new round of blisters to the arches
In stereo, round and round

You could feel your quadriceps
Locals and two-hundred Jewish kids
The seniors and the waiters
Got to go to Fenway Park and Montreal in '76
Mount Washington
In Portland I got to see the Marshall Tucker Band
Was I twelve?
Eleven?
I remember the flutes and tobacco voices
I sat with Scott and Sam
A group named "Frankie Goes to Hollywood"
    warmed up for the band
I can't believe I remember … the Portland
    Civic Center
*Damn…*

> *Oh the cow kicked nilly*
> *In the billy*
> *On the farm*
> *Oh the cow kicked nilly*
> *In the billy*
> *On the farm*
> *Oh the cow kicked nilly*
> *In the billy*
> *On the farm*

*And the old farmer said*
*Won't do no harm*
*Next verse…*


And cross my heart, hope to die
Seven years bad luck and a stick in the eye
I witnessed a Sasquatch
An actual bigfoot
Me and Sammy
It had pointed ears
Walked fully upright
Right by the forest in back of our bunk
A fuckin' bigfoot!
It was early evening
We were in our shower robes
And there it was
Walking as a man and growling 'neath its breath
We listened for a second
Just before me and Sammy bolted across campus
Naked as the day we were born
Scared to death
And no, it wasn't Bobby Sadowski
And no, it wasn't Lou Singer
Neither was it that red-haired fellow, Rufus
And no, it wasn't Phillip Korn

Oh, I go back to that camp in my mind sometimes
Beds were made
We swept our spots
Those storms came right down
Over our flagpole at Pleasant Lake

And I'd buy that land in a minute
Whole
As it was
And I wouldn't change a thing
For Chief Samoset—for his own sake
Maybe I'd add some skateboarding, drum circles,
    and motorcycle maintenance
I'd make sure to find out
About those hotdog buns, too
So delicious!
Smokey picnic tables
Grass dry
Late July

Yeah, David Goodman could never get thrown in jail
For harboring some bad habit
That turned whatever 'smarts' he might've had, dull
Some of those guys drive trucks
Some of them graduated from The Wharton School
    of Business

Some have families
What they do with their lives today, I don't know
But camp costs money, too
Weren't we privileged?
The fortunate?

Well, Brian Bowers became a co-manager for the
    Philadelphia Phillies
He was the camp's best lookin' man
Had a smile like California
Half-blooded American Indian
And of course you're all acquainted
With Senator Josh Blum

Jack Osmond of that bunk 13
*Legendary!*
He's growing palm trees in Homestead
To put bread on the table
Jack's a lion amongst men
Has a family restaurant here in Coral Gables,
    Florida, too
Andy Zaron became an insurance lawyer
(Whatever they do)
He has a child or two now
With a pretty little brown-eyed wife to consider

Coach Collin Burgess
After teaching for a few years at St. Luke's College
He's now stateside
Tryin' to put some of that English magic
Into one athletic organization or another
Plenty of Brit pride
*Colin was the cure for homesickness*
*He loved you and you just had to love him back*

Cary DuPont is a sports editor for the
 *New Orleans Picayune*
Lives a quiet life in the French quarter
Was that him I saw at Mardi Gras howlin' at
 the moon?

Rob Lewis, our great Welsh tennis coach
Is rumored to have successfully gotten away
With several bank heists in the South of France
Also, it is rumored of the fine Welshman
That he runs a cheeky little monkey joint in Belgrade
They say he never keeps it in his pants

You've heard of that former NY governor
That Spitzer guy
He got pegged with some fine gal

Who went to our sister camp, Camp Vega
Her name was Goldsmith
Yeah, Jenny Goldsmith
She was the foxy one I was dancing with

The great human force
That kept Camp Samoset together
Gordy Vye
He passed on a few years back
Now, there was only one Gordy Vye
A man on top of things

Robbie Wolfson
After having a minor career in coffee vending
And doing a stint or two as a roadie for
    The Grateful Dead
He's now farming in the Carolinas
He keeps beehives
Grows fine tobacco
And I hear he has three "wife-a-linas"

So Sam Seder is still in radio
He's got a grip on all the liberal-minded
    intellectual stuff
That's wounded these days, teetering by

I've heard him
The more he tries to cover up that Boston accent...
He should run for President
By and by
Sammy used to pester and taunt the
    English counselors
About having lost the Revolutionary war
Then young Sam would plead with the blokes
To sing their drinking songs to him
One more time
Again and again
Before the summer was up
Sam would have those Pub songs memorized
Sam came from Worcester, Massachusetts
("Woostah!")

I don't know what's become
Of that Bryce Levitt guy
Or Sugar or Smiley
Or really any of them who were part of it all
But couldn't you just rent a car and drive to Casco
To just stand there in the heart of it?
Not deep in winter, mind you
But God, yes, to see those Maine woods in fall!

David Goodman was always so full of laughter
His hands plunged deep into the front pockets of
   his jeans
Kind
I'm sure he's full of soccer mom understandings
I guess he's just a "good person"
To his friends and his family
Thinking little of himself in things
A mensch
One fine Jew

I wonder what tides them all over?
Cartoons? Mickey Mouse t-shirts? Classic porn?
What is there to do in Connecticut?
Demanding wives
Euro vacations in J. Crew
I guess we're all busy building little geniuses
I guess we're all just busy being born

*Day is done*
*Gone the sun*
*From the lakes*
*From the hills*
*From the skies*
*All is well*

*Safely rest*
*God is one*


Every time I listen to Bob Dylan
Singing on his *Budokan Live* record
I remember where Scotty's tapes had recorded
The scratches from his sister Pam's vinyl
And Scotty sang sweetly on that canoe trip
I wonder if he remembers spontaneously singing
On a river's wide
"The Answer My Friend …"
We saw a golden eagle
Just above the treetops
On that canoe trip that was nearly our final


And to our camp directors
Wally and Steve and Foon and Fenton
And whoever else might have fed us those steak-
    ums…
We've much to thank you for
As do all of us who came and went from the region


This one time…
This one afternoon I heard some rockin' sounds
Come pumpin' from the rec hall

As I'm walking up campus from the waterfront
*Pumpin'*
I'm twelve … or eleven
Bryce Levitt had the camp's newly acquired
Boston Electronics killer sound system
At concert level!
Deranged he was in the rafters
"Hey little camper
Have you heard of REO Speedwagon?"
That's what he said as I was walkin' in
"This song is called "Roll With the Changes"
I stood there floored
Power
A moment remembered
*Man! Thundering*

I've been a lucky camper
Lived the life of musicians
Never worked a day in my life
Don't know what work even means

Now more about Bigfoot:
Too tall to be John Land
Like a burgundy-colored, cool walkin' man
Yes, Chewbacca

But not quite as hairy
Two pointed canines, and definitely sort of mean
I'm scaring myself a little right now
And I live in Pensacola
Everything's tucked in, comfortable, and clean
*Yep...*

Life's been good to me so far
So far life's been good to me
So let's make it one fall
We'll build a big fire down by the lake
Together again
That would be somethin'
Wouldn't that be great...?
Middle of it all

Much love, boys

—M.L.

# KINGS OF KOOL

Kings of kool
Kings of kool are quiet
Or up in a riot
Lit or suave
A rock is more ready to react
Just before push comes to shove

Kings of kool
Got all kinds of rage
Road rage
'Roid rage
Kings of cool cage rage

He's the king of kool
"Nice boots
Do they coil?"
Bet they came in a king sized box
With a Texas-sized bottle of oil

Saturday night special
Hollow bullet bad
Papa was a rollin' stone
Fire in a flask
Stash in a bag

A king of kool
He's in his own world
Every bit his own god
He has no idea how truly boring he is
You heard me cowboy
And you too, y' punk sod

Kings of kool
"Yeah, Teach"
A play called 'Grease'
He'll blacken your eye
He'll kick your dog
Sand in your face at the beach
*What'd you have to go and do that for?*
*God!*

Joe Cool
Hangin' by the water fountain
Behind those cool black shades
Does he come from a broken home?
Can he read?
Cheap gun
Switch blade

Born down in a dead man's town
First kick I took was when I hit the ground

End up like a dog that's been beat too much
Till you spend half your life
Just a' coverin' up, now[7]

The kings of cool
The queens of kool
Where all must be chic, caché
I'm comin' out so you better get this party started[8]
Yeah … like maybe someday

A multi-thousand dollar, diamond studded, con-
    toured dress
Yes, yes
Breathlessness
The newly inspired, starving female populace
Chic and caché
Now I'll get out of your face

It's not rocket science
What goes on in these groups
Just a new set of players
Jumping through a new set of hoops

Where's this Koolie gonna take ya?
He knows how to have a real good time
There's a whole half a cold turkey in the refrigerator

Every room has four basic walls to climb
A king of kool…
He's got a need to let you know
"What do you mean, 'you've got somewhere else to
    be,' baby?
What do ya mean, 'ya got somewhere else to go?'"

Kings of kool
The creampuff Casper, milquetoast
Too Tall Jones of a Ray Bob Lemon
He's a chapter you'd like to forget
Remembered less than the tattoo you're wearin'

A king of kool
He's in charge
He's the man at the top
His time may belong to someone else
He takes his breaks with the local Penthouse crop
The deep-tanned sugarbitch Penthouse crop

Even if he could retain some purpose
His vision is a tunneled thing
Always so misunderstood
Led by trouble
Trouble following

A king of kool
Freestyle
Radical at the microphone
I don't go out on the town to be hit by a hammer
And, bro, you don't know squat about Sly and the
    Family Stone
Booker T and the MGs
Or Johnny Cash in the Folsom County slammer

Kings of kool
The jousting and fencing events have been cancelled
On account of this unceasing wind and rain
All efforts are being made
To preserve the tournament's continuity and comple-
    tion
And as promised, lunch will be served on the upper
    mezzanine

Kings of kool
Sonny was the hothead
Michael was charged but discreet
No one was around the old man
When he caught it on his old Italian street

Arthur Fonzarelli
"Hey, Shortcake"

James Dean gave it to 'em on the first take
Henry Hill
Blue eyes on the corner
Donny Brasco, undercover
Clint Eastwood
Steve McQueen
Sean Connery
Roger Moore
From Angie Dickinson to Juliette Lewis
Glenn Close
Kate Blanchett
Mariska
Demi Moore
Jodie Foster
*Goddam, girl!*

Cool
Don't know which is worse
Doin' your own thing or bein' cool[9]
*How to Win Friends and Influence People?*
Jesus!
An actual title
A manual with directions
Essential rules
*How to Be a Fucking Snake!*

Thou shalt not envy
Thou shalt not covet thy neighbor's house
Nor covet thy neighbor's wife
Thou shalt not steal
Thou shalt not kill…
Kool one day comes to face its victim
Kool one day got to swallow its pill

# Swimming Tips

Relaxed breaststroke
Proper breaststroke kick (not flutter)
Ask the lifeguard to show you the proper kick
So you get a mental picture
Then it's yours! (You might already know it)
If you have to, ask the lifeguard again
That's what he's there for

If you smoke, start easy
You'll do two laps
Then catch your breath
The rest, try four

Catching your breath is a shallow-end activity
Rest, but don't stand still
Walk it off
Rhythm releases while stillness after exertion makes
   you dizzy
Tell the people who are friendly enough
To talk to their fellow swimmers
That the swimming hour is
What you do for *yourself*
"I'd love to continue our enthralling conversation
But, I'm here to fly"

Catching breath after each set:
Assume Sumo wrestler position in the shallow end
Don't worry; no one can see you underwater
Do double taps off each foot like a drummer would
Left, left, right, right
Left, left, right, right
Relax and fall forward
Repeat
Think aquatic *T'ai-chi*

Extend coccyx ever so slowly out behind you
(Feels good, doesn't it?)
Resume laps

The breaststroke is *mellow*
Keep shoulders and neck relaxed
We exhale when submerged
And inhale when emerged
Watch the first *Avatar* flick
There's a quick scene in a swamp
That illustrates almost exactly what I'm
    sharing here
Full extension of all limbs
Minimum force
Maximum flow

Scout out pools that have competition lanes
Seventy-four feet
YMCAs are inexpensive and clean
And public swimming pools aren't icky

(Did you know there's a swimming pool under the
   White House?)

Which would you take?
In this hand: one of those long, shiny convertible
   Bentley motorcars
Or...
In this hand: an envelope containing these instruc-
   tions?
Answer: Take the Bentley
Sell it and dig a pool
Yeah, baby!


Three swims a week *is*
Four swims a week *counts*
Five swims a week gets you the *crème brulee*

# BREAK ON THROUGH

Ain't a word you can say 'cept to break on through
Break on through to some other side
And that don't mean you should end up in France
In a lizard skin suit
Bathtub romance

Break on through like that halfback for the Lions
Yeah, like Barry Sanders did
Or Don Quisenberry
Throwing those impossible side-handers
Betcha never seen that, kid

Or Walter Payton, how he held the ball when he ran
You got to know it don't come easy on the gridiron
Power of a lion with the grace of a gazelle
Number 43
No jive to sell
And always a gentleman
Man, that was Walter Payton

Break on through
What could it mean to you?
The world is round the world is flat

Ma'am those are lovely dishes
But somebody's gotta dust 'em
And what do I need with that?
Strange as the fins on an Eldorado Cadillac

Break on through
Syncopated swimming at the Olympics
Last of the Mohicans
And other vital statistics
Break on through

Cards are no good
Don't know why
And wouldn't you know
There's no way around here to get high
Re-release of his struggle saw two trains collide
High on an alpine mountainside

Break on through to another side
Don't you cry
And don't you die
And don't you burn
Break on through to another side
The changing fingerprints of the entrepreneur
Tales of the roving gambler

Break on through
Think not diminutively
Break on through
It's easy to be consumed by envy
Break on through
That which is not commoneth don't last
Break on through
He sees your deeds
He knows your needs
Even before you ask

Break on through
Has it taken men ten-thousand centuries to split
   seven days in half?
Break on through
Jesus headed into the wilderness
When he'd had just that much more than *enough*

Break on through
It's not in reclusiveness
Anyone who can write couldn't write in peace
Maybe it's in a parallel universe?
Seems feasible to me
Not at all intellectually perverse
Good steward

Bad steward.

Things most untoward
Break on through
Things I'd like to do a few times a week from this
   day forward

And of course, it's in things proverbial
Some things seem undeservable
Pocahontas
John Smith
*Hiawatha and Me*
*The Giving Tree*
What can you do with wet matches?
We might put a tune to this madman's poetry

Break on through

# Rocky Balboa's Mom's Salon on 71st Street

I seen neon Dion Sanders the other night
All dressed in green
With two bodyguards
Moving down the sidewalk of the Ocean Drive scene

And there was Ellen Barkin
I had to stop when I saw that smile
I saw Cindy Lauper walkin' her dog in California
Peggy and Annie in New York City
Molly Ringwald on Miracle Mile

And one chilly bright winter's day
Billy Joel in a mid-length brown leather coat
He was with a maybe eight-year-old Alexis
I got pretty excited, but I didn't stare or interlope

I served that palomino John Oats of Hall and Oats
Some vegetarian food at a health food restaurant
I could not resist
I followed him out in the rain
I said to him, "John, You guys could cover that song
    by the Skylights:
'And if it Don't Work Out'"

I saw Spuds Mackenzie on my block
And Nipper the RCA dog, too
Shoot, I saw Hooch the other day on the beach
With Tom Hanks' niece in aviators
Well, how do you do?

And damn! I seen Benji runnin' free
And Rin-Tin-Tin lots of times
He can get mean
Lassie is a lot smaller in person
Than that collie appears on-screen

I once had a green and black-checkered shirt
Worn by detective Tubbs on Miami Vice
I never saw a single episode of the series
But I wore the shirt a lot
I look good in green
And the knitting was nice
(I might still have it)

One morning I was riding my blue Grace Jones
    scooter
When the movie, "Ace Ventura: Pet Detective" was
    being shot
That scene where he skids his beat up, piece of crap,
    early '70s Chevelle

Into that Washington Avenue parking spot
"Hello, Satan"
One rainy night by Lou's tattoos
Joan Baez came ridin' by
In a hard-top baby blue '64 Mustang
It's true, the Spanish age so well…


I smoked a joint with Nestor Torres one night at his
    gig on 6<sup>th</sup>
He's quite the flutist
And on Thunder Boat Row, there was a 60-foot
    mean, green machine
That belonged to none other than Mr.
    Lenny Kravitz


I had an uncle whose name was Maurice
We called him coincidentally, "Uncle Rocky"
He took the movie stars and baseball players of his
    day fishing
At the end of the Tamiami trail
Clear to a place called Chokoloskee
I have pictures of him
With Stan Musial, Mickey Mantle, Sandy Koufax
JoeDimagio, Clark Gable …
Word got out you called Rocky Weinstein in Miami
If you wanted to flyline for Snook or Redfish

Once I took a seventeen-hour flight
From Zurich to Capetown, South Africa
To visit a friend who had fallen ill
I went out for a walk, and around the block
Bishop Desmond Tutu was speaking to a flock
On the beach by a strange hotel down a hill

You know that guy Silvio from the Sopranos?
I was workin' as a courier delivering a package at
   the Century Hotel
And who was sittin' right there in his
   pajama bottoms
Eatin' parmesan and pears
But Steve Van Zandt, Miami Steve, Silvio
*Now* I've got a story to tell

Okay …
Nelson Wilbury, also known as Beatle
   George Harrison
In a 528i in Belgium
In a town where a Grand Prix race was being run
I didn't … I couldn't say a word
Like with Billy Joel, who'd been with his little
   Alexis
George Harrison was with Dhani, his young son

I know, I know it's unbelievable
But there was Keith Richards in a big black Mercedes
By the old Sun Trust building
By the Banana Republic on Lincoln Road
With a grand blonde lady

Of Kiss fame, there was Ace Frehley
Twice in that one summer
New York in June
He was also with a wild looking blonde with a choker
   on
He smiled as I was busking
And I quickly changed my tune ...

   *I ... wanna rock and roll all night...*

He walked by me in Philadelphia one day in July
After I'd just finished a tune

With a little girl grin
Sheryl Crow in a little Mercedes pullin' out of
   Neiman Marcus on a sunny day
I met Gloria Estefan and her husband
Their daughter was in the same dojo
Where my son was learning karate

Almost forgot ... I met Elton John at a racquet club
"Here's my tape; it's me."
He has a pretty good forehand, but a lousy serve
Have you heard that 70 is the new 40?
Really?


I met Dave Barry, the newspaper man
In an Italian restaurant in the Florida town of
    San Souci
We talked about Warren Zevon who had recently
    passed on
They were bandmates in The Remainders
The Rock Bottom Remainders
Dave Barry looks just like Dave Barry
*Try the arugula*
*The carpaccio's a specialty*


When I was a kid
I played tennis with Roscoe Tanner and John
    McEnroe
At the Miami Jai Alai Fronton ... once
And Aaron Crickstein at the Junior Orange Bowl
    tournament
He had me doing stunts
I played on a tennis court with the mustachioed
    Australian John Newcombe

I played at an old Jewish gangster's house
With 'The Bagel Boys"
Eddy Dibbs and Harold Solomon
*Fierce!*

Wearing a pressed white linen suit
Come walkin' like he come clean from somewhere
   far, far away
That had to be Tom Petty
I *swear* it was Tom Petty
I'd been listening to flamenco guitars at the Hotel
   Breakwater
He was kind o' tilted forward like he didn't
   weigh much
Blue-eyed and feather-steady

And there was Terrence Trent D'Arby in a
   white scarf
Champagne-colored Porsche 928 with gold mags
I walked by Mickey Rourke in front of the
   fifth Street Gym
He smelled like one of Angelo Dundee's boxing bags

And so, that brings us back to Sly Stallone's
   favorite salon
His portrait in every window of the place

Owned and run on Collins in '71
By his dear, dark-haired, sweet Italian mom

She must have been quite a looker
'Cause Sylvester Stallone ain't your average grouper
Nope…

Wait … there's more

I seen John Prine after a tropical squall
With one of his girlfriends on a bench at Polo park
That *had* to have been him
He asked me if I was workin' out my bones
Strange question
It was late afternoon — some time before dark

*Hmmmm…*
Anyone else?

I saw Kenny Aaronson in Philly
Gettin' on a tour bus
Sideburns and all
What a rush!

I'm Rick James, bitch!

James Brown!
James Brown!
James Brown!
James Brown!

# HARVEY WEINSTEIN
# (NO RELATION)

The Zodiac Killer, Lopez
Or was it Hernandez?
Might have been Rodriguez
Jack the Ripper held all of London hostage
And he didn't even have a last name
Bundy, Berkowitz
Daumer
Buffalo Bill
Living next to someone who is amiable
Pleasant
Composed
And criminally insane

Harvey…
Sexual exploitation would be the last way
To inspire the *best*
In each brilliant actress or actor
And what's this "I'm mad at God" shit on NPR?
What books of counterfeit philosophy have you
    subscribed to?
Violence and rape…
*That's* your excuse?
Something you're used to?

Shame ... you've earned it, mister
You got the part at your asking price of sixteen-
   million dollars
You belong to *me* now
That, or I'll give it to *her*

Different tent
Different desert
Different well

Different hands
Different clothes
Different time

Harvey Weinstein
No relation of mine

# FUCK

Fuck you
Fuck it
Fuck all
Fuckin' shit
Fuck me
The fuck if I know
Fuckin' dick
Fuckin' pussy
Fuckin' pussy-ass bitch
Fuck 'em
*The fuck?*
They got fucked
They went and got fucked up
When in doubt, fuck
Fuckin' asshole
Fuck that shit
Fuck off!
What are you, a fuckin' idiot?
Can you fuckin' believe this?
What the fuck…!
"Never fuck me, Tony"
I pretty much fucked myself
Chicken chocaine motherfuckin' 'cane
Fuck y' motha

Motherfucka

Fuckin' shithead

Big fuckin' deal…

What are you fuckin' handing me?

Is this fuckin' for real?

Are *you* fucking for real?

Dude … Fuck!

For unlawful carnal knowledge

Fuckin' sonofabitch

Fuckin' sick sonofabitch

Fuckin' loser

Fuckin' pariah

Fuckin' turncoat

Fuckin' voyeur

Fuckin' stoolie

Fuckin' horse rustler

Fuckin' copperhead

Fuck it's cold up here!

Fuckin' spy

Fuckin' politicians

Fuckin' imp

Fuckin' arthritis

I wish I hadn't fucked everything up like I did

How did all this lead to so much fuckin' trouble?

Big fuckin' trouble

Where did you fuckin' learn this?

Take a fucking guess

This would be the big fuckin' picture…

Feel like I been fucked by a train

Where the fuck are we?

I don't know where the fuck we are

We're so fucked up about color in this country

You have no fucking class

You fuck

You fuckin' fuck

The fuck if I know

That's a motherfucker, man!

I've heard some shit in my time,
    but this fucking tops 'em all

Fuck that

I don't fucking remember anything

I gotta get the fuck outta here…

Right fuckin' *now*

Don't you have some place else to be instead of stayin'
    here makin' a fuckin' fool out o' me?

Whoever's lighting off fireworks can come up to the
    stage and I'll give you your money back and you
    can get the fuck outta my show

Fuckin' pig

Fuckin' grease monkey

Fuckin' dipshit
Can you please watch your language!? Fuck!
If we bypass this gasket, it should
    unfuck the system
If they can't take a joke, fuck 'em
Fuck, that hurts!
Ok fuckhead, that's enough
Shut up, fuckwad
Fuckin' mimes
"You went to Miami?"
"Yeah"
"Did you go parasailing?"
"No"
"Why not?"
"I didn't go parasailing in Miami 'cause I thought
    I'd feel like a dumb, fucking, flying pig"
From now on, you're in fucked-ville
That's not fuckin' funny
Say "fuck" a lot, and don't smile; you'll get a lot
    of pussy
Really?
What happens tomorrow is on *your* fucking head,
    not mine
I stopped tryin' to make sense of everything a long
    fucking time ago
And you're fucking welcome

# I Danced and Sang

I danced and sang at the laundry today
I fed the jukebox for enough time to load the
   machines and be gay

Surprising, the selection
Buddy Holly
Van Morrison
R.E.M.
Eric Clapton
Ray Charles singin' "Who Cares" with Dolly Parton
Carlos Santana
Willie Nelson
Edie Brickell
Paul Simon
Bobby Dylan
(Greatest Hits Volume I)

I danced and sang at the laundry today
Just loud enough to draw the beat and give way
"Hey, you two don't mind if I dance through this way?
This my laundry
My name's Maiche"

"Thank God I'm a Country Boy"
"Bad, Bad Leroy Brown"
"And the Joint was Rockin'"
 Goin' round and round
"Here Comes My Girl" and "Don't Do Me
   Like That"
"The Dirty Boogie," baby—that's the Stray Cats
 Only a Gibson guitar sounds like that

"La Isla Bonita"
"Beast of Burden"
"Hop Around"
"Won't you take me to…? "

"I get knocked down, but I get up again
 You're never gonna keep me down
 I get knocked down, but I get up again
 You're never gonna keep me down."
 (Pissin' the night away…)[10]

Once I got my loads filled
I went and stood in front of the box
I rolled my shoulders and let myself get loose
A deep breath of detergent and Clorox

I looked at the tunes some more
I got on the 'good foot' all over the floor
Then I ska-stepped and hip-hugged right down
   the aisle
Closed behind me the bathroom door

Believe it or not
This laundromat has a pool table in the middle of
   the place
Some dudes were racking up
The TV on the wall showed a stock car race

The soot on the fans
The stains on the ceiling
There's a guy doin' his own dance in here
He's on key
He's got feeling!

I stood my ground and shook off the children
   laughing
Stalking the floor
Fluorescents zapping

One couple over there
Sitting ever more closely on the benches

She says, "I don't know
Is there a manager on premises?"

I sweated through those tunes with a break
To piss and get some more quarters
"Every Time You Walk in the Room"
"And Then She Kissed Me," by The Searchers

Daytime traffic
Clacking dryers
A repairman on his back with a fistful of wires

I danced and sang at the laundry today
Like that mad hoofer on the TV reel
Maybe you remember?
He had Doc Martins on
He's doin' a job on that stainless steel

I danced and sang at the laundry today
Cheer, Bounce, Shout and Gain
TV and billiards and potato chips
People Magazine and beautiful Latin chicks
¡Caramba!
Dang!

I danced and sang at the laundry today
Honey, I washed and dried
Now, you fold and put away
That *was* the deal we made

I danced and sang at the laundry today
Those people must've thought I was plum crazy
I danced and sang at the laundry today
See ya next week, eh?
Same songs, different day

# NEW AND NEWSWORTHY

The new hysteric
Adelle
The new criteria
Same empty shell
Same game, just up on a new level
My new address book
Look, it's electronic!
The new mark
The new edge
The new precedent
Olivia Newton John
Sam Kinison
The new waterline under the bridge
A new set of problems
Newbies
Newly twisted proclivities
A new bad habit
The new cast of characters
New shows this season
This year's model
Newly found wealth
He was granted a new trial
New Riders of the Purple Sage
Newt Gingrich

Danny Noonan
(The nymph's FILA tennis shirt had us wrecked
   for months)
New Greenwich Village
New Ipswich clams (by the dozen)
A new micro-brewery
*Hey, who wants another beer?*
The New Testament
The good news
New Jax City
My parents honeymooned in Newport News
(There was a hurricane coming)
Sir Isaac Newton
What's new?
I don't know; what's new with you?
The worst song Carole King ever recorded
Was for the soundtrack to *Working Girl*
It's title: "The New Jerusalem"
Big 80s drums and everything
Hey, who's the new guy?
Huey Lewis and the News
That guy doesn't sleep, does he?
How do you spell "nuisance?"
Now I'm in Cali making *new* friends
Peanut butter sesame noodles

A new century
The new millennium
He made his fortune painting nudes in 1803
Hardcore shit
They ate it up, man
There's nothing new under the sun
I feel like a new man
Paul Newman
It's a new day
A new morning
For Ganesh the elephant god
Each day is the beginning of something new
The new world order
New Wave
Newspapers
A new set of lies
Did you get a new haircut…?
And new shoes—what are they?
Neutron bombs are not good for children
And other creepy crawlies
Hey, there's a new sushi place
You snooze you lose
They found a working rescue dog—a Newfoundland
Swimming 275 miles offshore
The new Red Clay Ramblers

I got news for you, baby...
Oh yeah?
Eagle scouts must right a capsized canoe —
   if you didn't know
The things you learn you never knew!
My first new car
That new car smell
One of my immediate goals
Is to buy a dark-eyed gal
A like-new, completely overhauled, black MGB
   Midget convertible
Steppin' out of that
This shorty...
It just matches...
All over the place!
Brand spankin' new
A goat is a ram and a sheep is a gnu
I'd forgotten that; I just learned it anew
New low prices
New location
Same old custard and Italian ices
Every once in a while ya gotta buy a new mattress
Noodles — get on that, will ya?

# FULL HALF-A-ZAPPA FREAK

I'd like to thank my editor and friend
Mr. Dave Bricker
For helping me to process my poetry this year
   gone round
'16–'17
We both brought a lot to the table
My limping craft
And his literary and oratorical vaust
*Vaust?*
Our collaborative effort
Has been evenhandedly congenial
   and definitely fluid
I told him early I wouldn't let him take the piss 'n'
   vinegar outta my shit
I could not have asked for a better partner in rhyme
Although for the next book
I'm thinking I'll seek out
An overweight Ivy League type, frustrated, middle-
   aged female
(I'm not exactly sure why)
It was always easy
To enter his front door and get down to work
Just as it was easy to take a jazzy bluegrass break
Dancin' with the hounds

Man, I hope it never happens
But if someone ever breaks in
And steals your D-28...
Don't come lookin' for me!

Yeah, full half a Zappa freak
And I didn't even know it!
We cousins and we brothers, Brick
What a year!
Thanks
Big Love

— Maiche

# It's Rainin' in New Orleans

It's rainin'
It's rainin' in New Orleans
The drops come down like light bulbs breakin'
There won't be a reading tonight at BJ's lounge
"The stage is a raft," the emcee laughed

It's rainin' in New Orleans
It's rainin' cats and dogs
Floatin' down the street
Bus benches — painted logs

It's rainin' in New Orleans
Can't see across the street
It's rainin' in New Orleans
Jumped into the streetcar
Couldn't find a seat

It's rainin' in New Orleans
Lost my boots in the middle of the night
Somewhere down near Jackson Square
Looked down at my feet
Somethin' wasn't right

It's rainin'…
Rainin' in New Orleans
Everybody's back tire is stuck in the mud
The road han't been swept in fifty-five years
*We was jus' gittin' 'round to that…*
*And we don' need those pumps 'cause the rain does the job*

It's rainin' in New Orleans
The trees is dancin' with the wires
They'd a cut 'em back
But all the city had was a pair o' pliers

It's rainin'…
Rainin' in New Orleans
All the junkies knew it'd keep up
They could feel it in their veins

The Mardi-Gras saint found his throne was
    jus' a folding chair
The tap-dancers
Shirtless
Splashin'
Like they always do in the rain down there…
Down in New Orleans

Yes, it's rainin' in New Orleans

*Shorty…*
*Seems this dinghy needed fixin' when this dinghy needed*
*   fixin'…*
*Yeah, that's jus' 'bout what I's thinkin'*
*Shorty…*
*You know how to swim?*
*Yeah*
*Shorty…*
*Leas' it i'nt cold out*

*I like a lot o' places*
*But I Like New Orleans better*
*A girl came walkin' froim the shadows*
*Met a guy in a yellow crew-neck sweater*

It's rainin' in New Orleans
The Mardi-Gras beads
Tears of a clown
It's rainin' in New Orleans
The rain keeps fallin'
Fallin'
Fallin'
*Down*
*Down*

It's rainin' in New Orleans

# HA' T' GIT DOWN IN DAT WATER

Ha' t' git down in dat water
Move on d' rock 'n' sand
Ha' t' git down in dat water
Ha' t' git away from d' master man

Ha' t' git down in dat water
Put my po' beat body in
Ha' t' git down in dat water
Oh dat cold
It ain't foolin'

Ha' t' git down in dat water
Soon the spring will come
Ha' t' git down in dat water
Mama said dat's when d' river right t' run

Ha' t' git down in dat water
It git wide up at d' head
Ha' t' git down in dat water
Moccasins all up 'round my head

Ha' t' git down in dat water
White man jus' as drunk as he is mean
Ha' t' git down in dat water

We jus' as clean as you are
Jus' as clean

Ha' t' git down in dat water
Follow the drinkin' gourd
Ha' t' git down in dat water
Arm around dat log
Stay far far from d' shore

Ha' t' git down in dat water
Grease up on the bank
Ha' t' git down in dat water
Mama said I'll know the Chesapeake

Ha' t' git down in dat water
Wrap up 'n' store my chaw
Ha' t' git down in dat water
Cousin told me 'bout the soldja

Ha' t' git down in dat water
It ain't just *almos'* for real no mo'
Ha' t' git down in dat water
"You won' be comin' back here, son
To be free, you mus' endure"

# DETROIT LESLIE

Whoever invented the Hammond B-3 Leslie
   organ speaker
Must be an ally
Before all this I was a baffled numbers guy
And there are other fellas in there
Who have to come along for the ride, Jim
Before they called him 'Sweet Baby James'
He was known as 'Mudslide Slim'

There isn't any reality to any of this
Waiving goodbye sittin' atop a sack of
   wildflower seeds
To dance, y' need a clear conscience
A clear conscience is what y' need to dance
   (pretty much)

"Jitterbug Waltz"
"Jitterbug Rag"
Chubby Checker in drag
Imagine having roomed next door to
   Charlie Parker or Stan Getz
Or Sidney Bechet, John Coltrane, or *Jesus!* —
   Keith Jarrett

The Hammond B3 Leslie…
An ally…
Blood of the church
Chains across the sky
Master Jimmy Smith
King Joey DiFrancesco
Prince Ray Manzarek
*Gimme some more names…*
Rick Wakeman of Yes
That guy from Kansas
B3 is everywhere in music
Someone a little twisted must have invented it
A guy named Donald Leslie
*Respect!*

What else would you call it?
Garth Hudson with The Band
He travels with an 800-pound organ
John Lord, the Deep Purple guy
And in a thousand little chapels nestled in the pines
Or in a second-hand music store in Detroit
Ray's Music Exchange
*Boy, she spins jus' fine!*
*Good action!*
*'N' I'll give y' a good buy…*

*I know ... I know ...*
*I'll put 'er on layaway!*

Dec. 23, 1952     D. J. LESLIE     2,622,692

APPARATUS FOR IMPOSING VIBRATO ON SOUND

Original Filed July 9, 1945

INVENTOR.
DONALD J. LESLIE,
BY
*John Flam*
ATTORNEY.

# THAN LISTEN TO THIS 80's CRAP,
# I'D RATHER...

Twenty-five years from now
You'll walk through your local market
Only to hear "Tainted Love"
For the 600th time in your life

I'd rather swim with sharks
I'd rather deliver the mail
I'd rather take a vow of silence
I'd rather live in a tent
I'd rather move to China
I'd rather recognize *your* side of the story

*There is always something there to remind me...*

I'd rather stand all night in the pouring rain
I'd rather stare at the ceiling for like, hours
I'd rather have a rich man's woman to please
I'd rather run out of my meds
I'd rather eat cigarettes
I'd rather get caught in a porn theater
I'd rather step on a black Adriatic sea urchin
I'd rather bowl

I'd rather get in the habit of falling asleep
    with the TV on
I'd rather get hooked on General Hospital
I'd rather get addicted to something that makes my
    teeth soft
I'd rather watch Lawrence Welk with my mother
I'd rather find out that comedy isn't pretty
I'd rather vape

*Get to know the feeling of liberation and release*
*Hey, now*
*Hey, now*

# FEATHERWEIGHT IN POUNDERVILLE

Masturbation
It ain't just a thing of the genitals
Masturbation knows many forms
Ethics, morals, purpose, principals
You can masturbate with a pencil and a pen
  on the page
You can masturbate all over the political stage
A baboon will do it in his cage
Whatever works for him
Pent up rage

You can masturbate in front of 27,000 adoring fans
In front of a congregation
An echoing stadium … Dinner Key auditorium
On television
On the radio
A peep show
Autoeroticism

Got it?
Flaunt it
Walking down the runway
Head held high

She's arrived
Hell on heels
*It don't get any better than this, kids*
Skin and bones
Super model status
Sneering at us
New York
LA
Milan
Paris

Belly button ring
Botox eyes
Injected lips
Lipo hips
Money shot
Silicon tits
The very acceptance of all of this…

I remember her
We made love from ten miles away
Variations
Xavier Hollander
*Forum*
I remember her…

Just yesterday we passed each other
And looked the other way

They're called 'babes' in America
In England they call 'em 'birds'
Nuno Bettencourt's black fingernails
Singin' "More than Words"

Somehow someone's got her arms wrapped 'round
    her legs
Cryin' in the shower
Sex sells, man
And for fifty cents
You can close the door and buy a thrill
Fifteen minutes into rush hour

Get sucked into a freak show
In San Fran
New Orleans
Thailand, too
Entertain the strange
The tantric will hold nothing for you

*Talk Dirty to Me*
*The Education of Misty*

Fishnet
Heels
As a teen I watched the same movie 950 times
  (or thereabouts)
Modesty…
Naturally we cover up
If you look, there's a lot of paid rape on the screen
That's not pleasure
That's just plain mean

I've been there
*Doesn't anybody knock anymore?*
Oh, you've got a pair!
When I was seventeen
I hired an escort
*No, not a whore*
Got a blister on my lip
Had to go see my doctor

Here, Mr. Jones
Take this pill
It'll do wonders for your love
And your heart
*Sure, it's safe…*
And your wife will sleep like a baby
Like a dove

Fantasy of opulence
Fantasy of violence
Youthfulness
Incest
Rich or poor
Straight or gay
The bottom of the barrel
Pizza boys
Car wash toys
Gangbangers
Police officers
Anything goes
It's all fucking okay
I was enjoying one just the other day

*You'll go blind*
*You'll grow hair on your hands*
He's angry and miserable
Kleenex in a ball
She puts down the phone and gets busy when I call

Give me cocaine
Feed me some bourbon
I'll need somethin' to do
And I'd be lyin' if I said I never took some
    comfort there

I'd tell you more…

But it's none of your goddamned business

Who the hell are you?

# PRINCE ROGERS NELSON

In the dark
Light shooting up from a crater-like crevice
In stone earth moonscape
In the light
He was reaching to plug in
Perfect he
Painted in low-lying clouds
Above

And at a bed stand lamp
In a motel room
At the sleeping hour
Door slowly closing
"Are you comfortable, Prince Rogers Nelson?"
"Good night, Prince"

A year it has not been

# I NEED TO THANK THE LORD

I need to thank the Lord
I say…
For what and in what ways
Have I held myself apart?
I need to thank the Lord for showing me
I could find a way back
Into what I so loved from the start
Thank the Lord for showing me
What lurks within the human heart

I need to thank the Lord
Thank Him for these eyes and ears
Thank Him for all the little things
We grow so entirely used to
Throughout our years

I need to thank the Lord
For remaining faithful to my soul
For the longest time
It was the little things
That regained control

Oh, me
Foolish enough to waste time

Trouble in mind, Lord
Trouble in mind
What was lying in wait there?
Spiritual warfare

Trouble in mind, Lord
Trouble in mind
Thank you, Lord
For helping me deal
With what's been more than a man can bear

Trouble in mind, Lord
Trouble in mind
I guess it's up to me
Which road to take from here

# MAHALIA

Mahalia, Mahalia
Your daughter not at home
Mahalia, Mahalia
Your son playin' all alone
Mahalia, Mahalia
At play in the fields of the Lord
Mahalia, Mahalia
The thread, the cocoon, the gourd

Mahalia, Mahalia
Only you could know
Mahalia, Mahalia
A dirt-poor puppet show
Mahalia, Mahalia
Search me; search me out
Mahalia, Mahalia
Dust of a plague blown from a drought

Mahalia, Mahalia
Your voice; not theirs
Mahalia, Mahalia
Your own kind, blind, gone debonair
Mahalia, Mahalia
Stranded, puttin' on airs

Mahalia, Mahalia
They've only got what's theirs

Mahalia, Mahalia
How much longer … this bag of tricks?
Mahalia, Mahalia
Mahalia bear witness
Mahalia, Mahalia
They've all got names
Mahalia, Mahalia
Wolves and thieves the same

Mahalia, Mahalia
The Southern Cross
Mahalia, Mahalia
For the fortress
Mahalia, Mahalia
It was all colored blue
Mahalia, Mahalia
It was just that big; it didn't know what to do

Mahalia, Mahalia
There was nothing underneath
Mahalia, Mahalia
What we lose for tryin' to keep
Mahalia, Mahalia

I am the luthier's friend
Mahalia, Mahalia
The drums of morning

Mahalia, Mahalia
The stiff naked man
Mahalia, Mahalia
There's brass in the sand
Mahalia, Mahalia
Cotton in the wind
Mahalia, Mahalia
Jerusalem

Mahalia, Mahalia
Laughing fires
Mahalia, Mahalia
Your churches; your choirs
Mahalia, Mahalia
Demagoguery
Mahalia, Mahalia
So much you wouldn't want to see
Mahalia, Mahalia
Come pour some sugar on me

Mahalia, Mahalia
Mahalia, Mahalia

# BECOME A SINGER

Become a singer
It melts people's hearts
Country boy sings country
City boy got street smarts

You can always keep a singer softly humming in
    your pocket
"Mississippi Half-step Uptown Toodle-oo"
Linda Ronstadt on roller skates there in a locket
She belted her way through an octave or two
Linda Ronstadt
FM
Waddy Wachtel was her man
Warren Zevon's *still* writing songs about her
In Rock 'n' roll Heaven
Linda Ronstadt
Limited edition

There's a singer at the roadhouse
People have a real good time
Didn't know they could
You don't know Bap Kennedy
You don't know Paul Brady
Mike Scott sang "Fisherman's Blues," *He did, did he?*

And he sang "Whole of the Moon"
"How Do I Love You?"
"Spirit"
"Your Love is Like Trumpets"
And "This is the Sea"
"If I Know You You'll Bang the Drum Like
    Monkeys Do"
"All the Things She Gave Me"
Sinead
Each of these
My three babies
Lourdes
Rockin' "Stars"
I'll have you just the way you are
"I Will Follow"
The Irish
They sing!

You get better
Stronger
Sweeter
Looser
*Vocal*
The Beatles cut their teeth in Hamburg
And killed it in Liverpool
Their harmonies instrumental

"In My Song"
Jah is the melody
*Oh-wah*

In my song…
"I've Learned Some Lessons in My Life"
There is no song so sad
As the sound of the man
Who does so cry
If I'm a truthful man
I love truthful people
If I'm an aggressive man
I love aggressive people
If I'm an intelligent man
I love intelligent people
I'm an awful man
And I love awful people
I've learned some lessons in my life[11]

A singer's been cryin'
About somethin' deep down
Somewhere in the second set he may smile
Raise his glass
He lives in a world full of willin' ladies
Poor boy can't touch a single lass

Wasn't it the greatest joy
To sing a new song
In the back seat of your family's car?
"Rockin' Robin"
"Mother and Child Reunion"
On the way to get new sneaks
At Suniland Mall

> *I'd like to teach the world to sing*
> *In perfect harmony*
> *I'd like to buy the world a Coke*
> *And keep it company*

Van Morrison sure gets you singin', don't he?
With Carlos Santana
You can share some Tibetan Yak tea
Prince said, "With one note, that man
Can lift you outta your seat"

> *And it stoned me to my soul,*
> *Stoned me just like goin' home*
> *And it stoned me…*

Become a singer
The fierce shriek of a hawk
Echoing down the canyon walls

Become a singer
They toss their panties
They lose their minds in the screaming
  "Me! Me!" calls

Become a singer...
A child in her room, humming
The next door neighbor's high decibel drumming
Across the canal
They turned it up to ten
I was a child under five
Steve Miller still drives me crazy
And that early Zeppelin...

  *Raise your voice in song*
  *And make a sweet sound*
  *Sweet sound*
  *Raise your voice in song*
  *And make a sweet sound*

Windows open
Windows closed
A knock on the door
They've been here before
Have a brownie, neighbor
And we'll play a little more

Some singers work real hard at it
But they can't shake the dread
That dread of the purest of notes mid-song …
That note that was inspired
And caught fire
While the recording button was on
That magic day back in '71

Some folks like to get away
Take a holiday from the neighborhood
Hop a *flight* to Miami Beach
Or to Hollywood

I've seen all the movie stars
In their fancy cars and their limousines
Been *high* in the Rockies under the evergreens

Gettin' it out like Joe Cocker
Like Aretha
Like Frankenstein
Gettin' it out on the bus
Or later in my room
Singing can change your mood
I'll be having a mood swing soon
Gettin' to the stage on time
Looks like we made it

I get by with a little help from these friends of mine
Become a singer
It melts people's hearts
Sometimes singers sound too rehearsed
But they're just warming up
Breakin' the ice
In walks a record executive with his nephew
"Whaddya think, Johnny?
Hit material?
Put it on the air?
Think it flies?"

# RUBBED Y' WRONG

I've rubbed y' wrong, friend
I've rubbed y' wrong
Y' prob'ly feel like I don't deserve to sing a song
I've rubbed y' wrong

What a rare and copacetic gift
Your company has become
"Dancin' in the moonlight"
Was Jerry Garcia's all-time favorite song
I guess I rubbed y' wrong, friend
Guess I rubbed y' wrong
Must be I don't have access
To the wavelengths you're on
'Rubbed y' wrong
That's my Thing Two…
Playin' with my Thing One
If you marry for money
That's what you get, Madam
You expressed yourself quite impressively
I saw you on your bike
In your Yankees cap
Front row at the US Open

I've rubbed y' wrong, man
I've rubbed y' wrong
I have my moments like anyone
You know the artist type
When they're young, they're never wrong

I've rubbed y' wrong
Go on, tell me
I know you're not bluffin'
You're a friend of a friend of Mr. Nothin'
And I've rubbed y' wrong
Why don't you just come out once and scream it
Like in the song

I've rubbed y' wrong
Ding-Dong Daddy Ding-Dong
I'm convinced there are lapses in your
    very foundation
Chess, Bridge, Keno, Mahjong
All that "what" crap to string along
I guess it rubbed me wrong

Rubbed y' wrong
Daddy's in the corner
With the same three words
First, "sick"

Then, "insane"
Then it really hurts
Talkin' 'bout the universe
And how it really fucking works

I've rubbed y' wrong
I'm goin' to Acapulco
Elena *loves* my song
And Lila and Christa and Mirca
They give it up for a little sing-along
They think the world of me
My name's Dom Hemingway

And I've rubbed y' wrong
You got to please yourself
'Cause y' jus' can't please everyone
I went to a garden party
They said I didn't belong
Guess I rubbed 'em wrong

I've rubbed y' wrong
Y' prob'ly feel like I don't deserve to sing a song
And that's exactly where I choose
To end this darlin' little one
I've rubbed y' wrong
I must have been guilty of something all along

You just whisper it into my ear
Before I'll be movin' on
I'm sorry…
But you were always off-key from the introduction
Of every single fucking song
Now go!
Get outta here, devil
You'd better run

# MY OLD FRIEND RALPH

My old buddy Ralph
Ain't seen him in five and fifteen years
Every once in a while
I'd think of the way we were as friends
We let rock 'n' roll music fill our hearts
He lived down the block from me
On 44th and Meridian
He was the kind of kid who didn't say too much
But I swear … every once in a while
He had what I'd call a pristine touch

Much later on in our lives
I grew to appreciate his powers of perception
    and response
In our youth, we were always jammin' loud in
    his room
Through the afternoon
We'd read *Rolling Stone* and *Relix* out loud
In his family's New Jersey summer house

Talk about the real deal
Ralphie was stealin' his daddy's cigarettes by eleven
In later years he'd show up to school with shiners
    once in a while

Must 've pissed off the old man again
"Who's been in my Marlboro carton?"

His daddy was from New York City
But really, he and their family stemmed from tribes
   in the rough, dry desert
I stayed with them one winter
On the North Jersey coast
About an hour on the train from New York

It was a cold winter
And that big house you could not keep warm
They watched the Yankees religiously
The whole house woke up when a line drive
   was caught
They'd hug and congratulate each other
Like they'd just made history!

We met when Ralph's uncles came to Miami Beach
And opened up a record shop on old Lincoln Road
This was ten years before South Beach's renovation
When opening anything there was an immediate
   downward spiral
I don't remember what they called the place
But I do remember Ralph's uncle popping his head
   through the bedroom door

Record collection on the bed and floor
"Boys, this one is called 'Hard Promises'
Tom Petty's new one
It's goin' like hot cakes
Flyin' out the door
Flyin'

Ralph's dad ran a camera shop on the other side of
    Lincoln Road
Across from Big Daddy's
Up from the sporting goods shop, 'Mr. R'
They lived in a house down the block from us
They had a projection TV
And after school it was cool…
We watched dirty movies on their VCR
And we'd always be peeking out the window to see if
    his mom was parking in the drive
"Maiche, she's gonna be home soon and we've seen
    this a hundred times"
We were into Zevon by fourteen
Motley Crüe could stay on Sunset Drive

Now Ralph always had some fine duds on his back
In New York his family was tied to the textile
    industry
Half a floor in the middle of the city

Family ties with Nic Nic shirts and Sassoon jeans
  and those shoes called "Candies"
In school, certain girls dug Ralph
They did
And he'd get into fights at lunch
He had some acne like me
He was a bad little rag-a-muffin in Armani


I was one of the neighborhood drummers
We'd all been blown away seeing Springsteen
  one summer
We'd get together and play in the guitar player's
  garage on Lakeview
Endlessly we'd play basic blues patterns
And then endlessly we'd play more blues patterns
That's what we'd do
We knew half of "Tattoo You"
And "Squeezebox" by The Who
Credence Clearwater
Buffalo Springfield
The Band, Bowie and a few originals got through
And yes, that Tommy Tutone number, too


Some of our parents had been hippies
And some not
We came to the glory of music by way of album-
  oriented rock

Fender
Gibson
Guild
Gretch
Peavey
Roland
Premier
Ludwig
Yamaha
Slingerland
Lee and Jordan and Ari and me
Sean and Joel and Matt and Miles and Frank and
   Manny
"Who'll Stop the Rain?"
Dylan's "Hurricane"
"Y' Say it's Your Birthday!"
Some Elvis rockabilly
"Suffragette City"
Purple Thai Stick
Sticky
Little Robbie Weiss with some of that Miami yellowy


People thought Ralph was less than gifted
Because he couldn't be bothered with books and stuff
He'd watched *The Godfather* six-hundred times
And other ultra-violent shit that blew you off
   the couch

One time my parents found half a Quaalude in
my bathroom
And when confronted I laid it on *him*
Everybody commits some kind of character-
crushing, unconscionable sin
Maybe even a second, my friend

He'd taken some weight off of his uncle's stereo
And had himself a mixer to DJ
We got together with it and I remember buying
him out
His family was moving back up north for greater
opportunity

Anyhow, however, cliques turn
I remember that Ralphie once in a while
Made it over to our rhythm and blues pit
I remember him standing there
Everyone fifteen years old
"What should we get on the pizza?"
Yeah, standing there with his arms folded
Leanin' back on the counter lookin' on
Listenin'
Peter Gunn into "Sloopy, Hang on, Yeah, Yeah,
Yeah, Yeah, Yeah, Yeah, Yeah"

When Ralph's family moved away
Ralph was to start the eleventh grade
He'd call me sometimes and ask me what I was into
What I'd been doing
I guess he was kind of lonely and sad
When you're young, you're in the big city's way
He always had a fresh bag of weed
He was kind of an outlaw
I was college bound and going
I remember asking him if he'd read out loud from
    *Rolling Stone*
And he'd start reading with full expression
Like me, he's probably got a drawer full of songs
All dealing with what it is to be a man amongst men


If he was dead I'd have heard it
And if he was in jail I'd know it
He may be a rich man
He may be poor
I'm sure he's come to wonder what it is a lot of people
    are living for
I seen him once in a dream
Squeezin' all the life out of a fifth fret major chord
Maybe someday we'll flesh out some vitality on a
    travelin' gypsy tour

Can't tell your best buddy that you love him
Can't pan for gold where there is no brook
You won't find the sweet grass in the state
   of Montana
Unless you know just where to look

Hope you're relaxed enough to kick off a tune
   on key
"This guy's pretty good" said the redhead standin'
   next to me
If you wanna buy a banjo we can go walkin'
We might get away with a lot less talkin'
Wish I'd learned to play the guitar
Wish I'd learned to play them drums
Howdy, East Orange, we got a late start
California, here we come
Paperback in his jeans pocket
Slept in the farmhouse under the stairs
Haven't seen my old buddy Ralph in five and
   fifteen years
Five and fifteen years

# VIRGIL, QUICK COME SEE
# (SPLASHDOWN)

These blue eyes
Your brown eyes
Emerald green
Hazel
Astrid
Golden orange autumn red
She was going to Ontario
Asked me if the highway was up ahead
Two days later, Levon Helm died
I'd have been halfway to Canada with a co-ed

Short scruffy raspy dudes
Will I always be this smart and handsome?
At the gates of heaven a drummer boy drums

Fine prince
You are made of rhythm
Rhythm and the sounds you tapped out
Rest, Levon
Rest, Levon Helm
Prince of the north
Son of the south

And there was never any doubt
That what you guys did
Will remain in rotation
Irresistibly
Forever

*Virgil…*
*Quick…*
*Come see!*

# WHAT DO I WANT FOR MY BIRTHDAY?

What do I want for my birthday?
Well, you know, I think I could use a truck
That'd be okay
You know it's hard to swipe stuff with just a bike
Mark Twain said, "Don't steal anything you can't just
    take away from plain sight"

That'd be all right
That'd be okay
Hooray!
You guys pulled together and bought me a truck for
    my birthday!

What do I want for my birthday?
How 'bout a fat gift certificate to my favorite record
    store…?
That'd be okay
For my nieces, some Psychedelic Furs
Something to liven up their day
Gotta get some Red Clay Ramblers, too
Seen 'em at the Stephen Talkhouse one time
Throwin' back a few

That'd be all right
That'd be okay
Hooray!
Generation Records
Imports for my birthday!

How 'bout a great big brown xylophone
Made with Madagascarian gourd?
My Lord!
I'll need a half-decent PA system
And some size-10½-D Italian tap shoes to twist in

And I want a unicycle
And three wishes
And twelve new harmonicas
And a machine to do my dishes!

What do I want for my birthday?
I want to take you out for sushi…
That'd be all right
That'd be okay
The ginger clears the pallet
Then some warm sake

That'd be all right
That'd be okay

*Ooooh wee…Oshitashi!*
Some of that off the small of your back
Happy, happy birthday

What do I want for my birthday?
Well, all that I've mentioned so far, and…
And…
And I'd like world peace
And I'd like more John Cleese
And Jamie Lee Curtis
And Patricia Arquette
Penelope Cruz
Patagonia sunset

And…
A table that's set
For two
Me and you
And next week, another birthday, too
Pick you up in my Chevy
We'll go down to the levee
Where some good old boys are drinkin' wine
   and whiskey

And I'd like a puppy
And some money

And a maid to clean this scary microwave
And anything I might think of between now
   and then

That'd be all right
That'd be okay
Never a day past forty
That's what I say
And that's what I want for my birthday

And a secretary who types
And a couple of cartons of Marlboro Ultra Lights
And I'd like to take my son to the movies
We'd get some Chinese spare ribs
Or pizza with pineapples and anchovies

Did I mention a stereo?

And I'd like there to be a world religion channel
And I'd like the child pornography posters taken
   off the bus stop panel, Bebe

And that's what I want for my birthday
Happy birthday, Maiche
Thanks, what'd you get me?

# To Those Few Brave Men at Resurrection Drums:

I, Mister Maiche Lev of Miami Beach …
Y' know, boys
I have recently robbed a string of banks across
   Alabama and Mississippi
And uh — nobody got hurt or anything …
So uh …
I would like delivered to my new home studio door
The following items:

* One green-stained, thick-shelled "D.W. Bonham"
  kit (You know the one)
* Those heavy and light Zildjian finger cymbals
  Made by Avedis in old Constantinople
  And played in the Sultan's Janissary band, please
* Some "anks" bells
  Purple braid *(big pussy magnet)*
  Made by the same company
  A whole box
  (Before Christmas, fellas!)
* Two tambourines:
  One, once held by Linda Ronstadt
  The other, a Stevie Nicks remnant

- Congaii
  Mahoganii
  With Giovanni Hildalgo's sweat stains on
  the skins
- Drum lessons
  With Cindy Blackman if she's available
- And some big-ass marching drum sticks
  (No brushes)
- Well …maybe some brushes *(thwack)*

Now …


Out of general personal self-disdain
For my newfound wealth — my ill-gotten gains
I intend to make full *e pluribus unumization*
By assuming the humble occupational position
Of sidewalk-dancer-with-"Drumzz"-sign dude
*Yes, I like it!*
I'll blow whistles dressed in costumes
I'll dance Reggae
Sing all day
I'll maintain corporeal hydration
And I'll eat phatt pastrami sandwiches with the
   Amtrak Howler blowin' by

*Turn here, bitch!*
*Rezz Drumzz*
*Hey, Jackass!*
*Don't you play?*
*Rezz Drumzz!*

I'll need the following outfits:

- Pirate
  With tri-cornered hat
  Eye patch
  *Live* parrot (Norwegian Blue, please)
- Great Ape
  (Monkeys are so peaceful ...
  But if you disturb them, they go apeshit!)
- Dumbo the Elephant
  *Loxodonta africana*
  (sans license from Disney)
- Football player
  Quarterback
  Cheekbone paint
  Cleats and helmet
  A cooler full of Gatorade (green only)
- Gangsta Rap Hoodlum
  Bling, cap, chains, exposed underwear,
  contemptuous stance

- Hippie dude
  Bag, bong, brownies, bottled water, and
  Birkenstocks
  Amen!

Boyz,

Aside from Ponzi schemes and bank heists
These days I actually have two humble places
    of employment
One of my bosses goes by the name of Ren
As in "Ren's Tarzan and Jane Landscaping"
Anyhow, fellas …
Ren is also a drummer in a slicing little girl group
    called "Jam Sandwich"
She's in and out of your store on a regular basis
    for supplies
Or was, at least
See, in a not so distant, recent past
One of you longhairs expressed a sudden certain
    shock and dismay
At one of Ren's children on the drum store floor
Yes, Ren is a mother of two young gifts unto
    the Universaii
Savannah, beyond seven, now
And Jeremiah, just past five

"Oh Ren,"
I said from the passenger seat in the cab of her work-
  ing Ford pickup
"Ren, Resurrection Drumzz has got the Ferrariaii
And the Lamborghiniaii of drum kits in there
Kids running around loose ...
With sticks?!"

"Ren,
I've been in and out of that store
Since the showroom space wasn't much larger
Than the two parking spaces out front ...
(And there used to be this Rush freak named John ...
  and ...
But that's a long story unto itself)

"Look Maiche," Ren replies
"I'm sure all that's true about kids and sticks
But they don't have to be nasty-like to my kids
I'm not their friend anymore"

"Oh, Ren ..."

So, y' Rezz boys,
Perhaps you should install a buzzer?

No, not a TASER!
  (Did you know that TASER stands for Thomas
      A. Swift's Electric Rifle?
  It's another long story…)
  *Now back to showroom floor child behavior*


How about a honking chime?
Yeah, a kind of a honking chime…
By the register
Good name for a brass band: "The Honking
    Chime"
*Damn, I'm good!*
Or, at least I'm working at it
On a regular basis
With a metronome…
(Some of the time)
    I am Mick Fleetwood's distracted eleven-year-old
        nephew, once removed
    *Bam!*


Brother Ali comes down from the office
"Hi, kids
Wanna play?"


And here comes Eddy

"Look here, Junior
This seat turns; it swivels
Can you say "swivels?""

Evan smiles and says
"Ho, ho, ho
To the tambourines we go"
Daryl is, of course, talking quietly on the telephone
And Ike needs to be walked

Jeff Lee comes down
With that *cafecito* rocket fuel
"Does anybody here know any bird noises?
How about a cockadoodledoo!
*Cockadoodle doooooooooooo!*
*Good!*
Now, how about some farm animal sounds!
*Good!*
And the piggie goes … *oink*
And the horsie goes … *neigh*
And the sheep says … *bahahah*
Now, Jeremiah, spin…!

Kids and drums
Kids and drums and their mums
We'll make millions!

And you can go my bail...
After Ike's been walked

# GO MICKEY!

There goes Mickey Erinson
He's playing with the horn again

*Hmmmmmmmmmmmmmm*
*Hmmmmmmmmmmmmmm*

There goes Mickey Erinson
He's playing with the horn again

*Hmmmmmmmmmmmmmm*
*Hmmmmmmmmmmmmmm*

There goes Mickey Erinson
He's playing with the horn again

*Hmmmmmmmmmmmmmm*
*Hmmmmmmmmmmmmmm*

There goes…

It's his boat, man!

*Hmmmmmmmmmmmmmm*
*Hmmmmmmmmmmmmmm*

# OH NO, OH NO

The staples in the teabag in the microwave oven
Oh no, Oh no, Oh no, Oh no
The staples in the teabag in the microwave oven
Oh no, Oh no, Oh no, Oh no


If it wasn't f' my mama or my dealer, this phone
   wouldn't never ring
Oh no, Oh no, Oh no, Oh no
If it wasn't f' my mama or my dealer, this phone
   wouldn't never ring
Oh no, Oh no, Oh no, Oh no


The ice machine doesn't have filtered water
Oh no, Oh no, Oh no, Oh no
The ice machine doesn't have filtered water
Oh no, Oh no, Oh no, Oh no


Up and down, little Jimmy, not side to side
Oh no, Oh no, Oh no, Oh no
Up and down, little Jimmy, not side to side
Oh no, Oh no, Oh no, Oh no

That never happens…
Oh no, Oh no, Oh no, Oh no
No, that never happens…
Oh no, Oh no, Oh no, Oh no

I'm hidin' from the mailman and I hate to hear the
    telephone ring[12]
Oh no, Oh no, Oh no, Oh no
I'm hidin' from the mailman and I hate to hear the
    telephone ring
Oh no, Oh no, Oh no, Oh no

Went for a walk in the pourin' rain
Oh no, Oh no, Oh no, Oh no
Don't think I'll ever be the same again
Oh no, Oh no, Oh no, Oh no

The staples in the teabag in the microwave oven
Oh no, Oh no, Oh no, Oh no
The staples in the teabag in the microwave oven
Oh no, Oh no, Oh no, Oh no

# PUNK

Punk rock was a brief phenom
Anger
Tantrum
"Black Market Clash"
Joe Strummer was a man with somewhere to go
In his motorcycle jacket
Guitar case at-hand
These laughable *monsters* out there now
Who's got the best Halloween costume?
Who's sound is most savage?
Where's my pigeon?
Gag me


And that *Rolling Stone* magazine
Did not put Joe on the cover at the time of his death
Is and forever will be a mark
On whatever that corporate rag might claim to
   stand for


*Alright Jonesy, do it again!*


This is England!
This is how we feel!
  -#! -#! -#! ZZZ -#=-# ♪ \\//@ -#! ZZZ -#...

# SOME OF TOM PETTY'S OTHER GREATEST HITS

"Dreamville"

"Blue Sunday"

"For All the Wrong Reasons"

"Ways to be Wicked"

"It'll All Work Out"

"Dogs On the Run"

"Runaway Trains"

"Self-made Man"

"She's Gonna Shine Forever"

"Swingin'"

"Louisiana Rain"

"Complex Kid"

"Ankle-deep In Love"

"The Best of Everything"

"Mary Got a Brand New Car"

"No Reason to Cry"

The Heartbreakers' rendition of "Hang On, Sloopy" redefines fun

West Palm Beach Aditorium, 1981

Did "Southern Accents" even get airplay?

Rest in Peace, Tom

You don't get to where he got to from where he started out unless you have something to prove to someone who's not listening to you.

—Jann Wenner, *Rolling Stone*, October, 2017

# SHIRA A

Shira
She comes together
Of light
It's daughter
Of night
Her father
Onyx gleams
Then gave was she
Then blessed were we
Shira

She's the world's cheekiest Monaco monkey
The remnant of a people
Stone of a living ancestry

She's an eight-year-old…
No, six
Comin' to the table for breakfast
Sleepy in a *Lion King* bathrobe
She sits
Her mother asks her nicely
If she would please 'sit up'
Shira comes alive
Making sure her brother didn't really get the prize

She pours the milk carefully with two hands
Huge black eyes

She's just this shorty little Jewish girl
Who grew up a few doors down from me
She and her brother come knock on my door
  every Saturday
Like two Bedouin children
They'd never go away

Pony girl
Made of moonbeams
And her brother so much the same
The two of them
The tasty platters they brought us
There's something called 'chollent'
A goulash to make you *convert*
Chollent is religion!

It was her name on the Marquee
At the Oprah house that Sunday
Biscayne Boulevard, Miami
Off-color independent shows
Who's on her way…?

She hangs with reggae gypsies
If anyone's goin' somewhere, she's…
It drew a smile
Once at a party
I heard her talkin' up the glory of New Orleans
Curses like a sailor in a moment for fun
She's one of those thespians

When she was little she learned to whistle
And she never stopped
When she was *way* little
She'd go around chirping a lot
*Odd*
She'd chase down tunes with it
Down the block goes a little kid making music

She does community theater
Any triumph
The place is hers
My young neighbor
Her voice she keeps with her
A play writer, a songwriter
An actor
A singer

Hauntingly familiar
A short haircut's goddess
Step aside now…
When she figures out her divinity
Her contentment will be your only peace

The last time I stopped in to see them
*La madre*
It was her mother's birthday
Being amongst them is reaffirming of something…
They're Jewish
And it makes my heart beat

*Shira!*
*Habibi, how are you?*

# DOIN' SOUND IS DOIN' SOUND
## (FOR A PEACEFUL WARRIOR)

Doin' sound is doin' sound
Good work when you can get it, really
Mostly live clubs, late night downtown
Got a gig at a place in Miami they call Tobacco Road
Been sitting in the same place 96-odd years
And one night last September
My trip nearly brought me to tears
Nearly brought...
Nearly brought me to tears

On my way downtown
Telephone rang
Crazy Davey with this, that and the other thang...
Regular night for me
GMC equipped
Destination abode
The one and only Tobacco Road
Century ol'
*Back 'er in, a little more...*
*Perfect!*
*Hey, what's up Ketchup?*
(That's my boy, Danny Cetzuep)

Feelin' alright
South Florida night
Patch bay behind the board
I can sit in with my friends
Got my SG tuned and out of the case
Got my old telecaster and its cord

Microphones
Plugs
Monitors
Guitar stands balanced and checked
*One, two, two, two…!*
*One, two, two, two…!*
*One, two!*
A little drizzle wafts its way in
Thunderstorm threat

*Tarps!*
*Where are the Tarps?*
*Ketchup! The tarps!*
"Dude, I used them for my bed
And they went up in the fire"
*Dude, its raining!*
*Fuck!*
*Kill power!*
*Everything comes in*

*Dude, get Johnny...*
*Get on it!*
*Ketchup*
*Go make sure he ain't lost!*
*Lost!*
*Johnny!*
*Ketchup!*

Showers past
Florida Power and Light
Show goes on
Lina comes with my burger 'n' fries
There stands a frosted mug of beer
*Y'know it is a great song, "Cheeseburger in Paradise"*
Decent crowd
Really, rainy night
Think I'll have a poke
Singer songwriters everywhere
Showin' us which way to go

Hmmm
Where are my keys?
They were with the weed in my pocket
My keys ... are not here
My keys are not here... or there
Keys

Not in the plants near the electrical sockets
They're not in the slats—
The slats between the planks on the floor
By this soundboard
Not anywhere around the lower lip of this grungy
   back door
Not in the loo…
There reads the ol' Blue Standard
Every waiter and waitress has said "I'm sorry, mi
   Amor"
And nothing been turned in at the bar
*Whiskey Sour, Mr. Bartender*

I was here
And there
Wait … I went upstairs
They just *gotta* be around here
Or there…
Or fuckin' *somewhere?*
Let's see…
We moved every last speaker into the hall by the
   old cigarette machine
No keys
Nothing
Okay…

Ketchup come up to say
"Hey, maybe your friend in the Grove has a set?"
"Yeah, Davey 'Blue Eyes', why didn't I think of that?"

*Davey, sorry to call so outta the blue*
*Yes, I know it's kinda late*
*But, I've lost my keys*
*I'm at The Road*
*I'm doin' sound*

*Oh, you have a set?*
*You do?*
*Dude, I'm so relieved!*

"What d'ya know, he's got a set.
Hey Davey's comin'"
Rock on boogie chillun!
We're cool
I got a roach
Ya gotta clip?"

"Hey Davey, what's up?"

End of the night
Got the gear in the van

A hundred thanks to Davey and those cats who
   hung with me
Doin' sound
You're the first to get there
And damn near the last to leave

You'd think it was the drummer
But that drummer is playin' on a riser down under
Y' see, and it ain't over till all the lights are off
And the soundman says goodnight to the boss
He starts up his van … and…
He's off, right?

Everything's secure
Doors locked
Seatbelts latched
Turn the key
No!
Not a dead battery…
No…

It's 4:00 in the morning
In the heart of a Miami parking lot
It's 4:00 in the morning
Everybody out there has something sharp
To take what you've got

I've simply got to jump this battery
Custodian took the last bus
There's nobody...
Just nobody and me
Latin lovers devourin' each other
Wearin' those Guyaberas and Capizzios
Those stiletto pumps

*Hey...*
*How ya doin'?*
*My car's over there*
*I need a jump...*

Another huddled group of people
You just flat out know ain't got a car
I can't call Davey 'Blue Eyes' again
But I could walk to Bayside Mall
It isn't two miles away
Lock-up is that way
Over the neon bridge
This homeless bazaar

They carry knives
They carry guns
One amongst them don't feel good
And gots something to prove

It's 4:00 in the morning
*This is not my neighborhood*

I don't want to bore ya
But we got her started on jumper cables and spit
My long day's night's exit

Yessiree…
Speakers
Mixers
Cabinets and cases
I-95 gonna carry me home
With National Public Radio
And all the Lord's good graces
The look on my face is…

Quite a night it's been
First, those South Florida rains
Then burnt tarps
Then lost keys
Dead battery
So glad I'm on my way
Moving
Feel of my load rampin' up 95 North
I haven't mentioned that I worked a full shift today
It's been a whole day

Since I've seen a bed
I'm passin' my twentieth hour
Lookin' at my twenty-fourth
(But I'm not hurtin')

*NPR*
*Good morning, it's 5:15!*
*This just in*
*All your money is halved…*
*Ponzi scheme*
*Derivatives on indicatives*
*What's on Diane Rheem?*

The Syrians are mad at the Lebanese
Baghdad still does whatever she please[13]
Natives in New Guinea with gold in their teeth
Might mean something to you
Don't mean nothin' to me…[14]

 *Bah-boom!*
 *Flappidy-flap-flap-flap-flappidy-flappidy-flap-flap…*

*Holy shit!*
*Keep her straight*
*Right lane*
*Motherfucker!*

*Holy shit!*
*Motherfucker…!*
*Keep her straight*
*Blowout!*
*I've got a blowout!*
*Flappidy-flap-flap-flap-flappidy-flappidy-flap-flap…*

Stopped in the median
Can't quite believe it
You don't know the shape I'm in
Floorboard
Brake
Foot to toe
Relax now, y' know
Tonight I have eaten crow

What a deep breath is
I can handle this
I'm a problem solver, I am
Three children and a house
Seems everybody has a difficult spouse
Problem solving's my life
I specialize in strife
A problem solver I am
And not some backslidin' Sam

At my job on the isle
Someone always hands me something hectic
My boss could be Joan Rivers
*Look busy!*
The clock at times don't seem to tick
When Pierre Cardin's porch light needs changin'
I'm the one to change it
I know Oprah Winfrey
She's a workaholic
Her book's somewhere back there in this van
By the toolbox
Near the vise-grips

Miami town is speedin' by
A touch more buzzed than wired
A light rain
I'm on my knees
Thinkin' Harry Chapin's angel's
Could they be up for hire?

Is there a patron saint
For a humble guitar slingin', hard workin' man such
   as me?
If there is, Lord, could you?
Would you?

Have that angel look down over me
I'm your number one Beatles fan
Your humble roadie

On my back
Spare tire's toward the rear
Got my hexagonal crowbar right here
Did I mention it's raining?
I'm underneath a van
It's rocky
And no one's there to hear any bitchin'
   or complainin'

*Cats in the cradle, and a silver spoon*
If I strip this bolt my head will pop like a balloon
*When y' comin' home dad? I don't know when*
Car jacks make me a little nervous
And a fully loaded van....
This day has been heavier than…

Butterfly bolt
Three fourths metal
One fourth rust
I'm sweating
Psychically willing it not to strip
Upward thrust
This gravel must be givin' me a tattoo

The sun don't break till six thirty
Seems a long way past
Okay…
I gotta do what I gotta do

Darkest hour of the day
Last hour of the night
Take a deep breath, Tommy Chong
A deep breath is always alright

Asphalt
Headlights
Dope!
Lug nuts
On tight
End of my rope!
You could definitely say I was at the cusp of
    coming undone
Oh yes, y' could say it was a night for the books

If I had me a Triple-A card
*If* I had me one
The paycheck from the gig is in my
    glove compartment
Mr. tow-truck driver, forget it
Don't even slow down
You better run!

Now I failed to mention that during this
   tire change
I couldn't cut the engine
I couldn't shut her down
Not with a dead battery
The exhaust
Bad headache comin' on

First work
Then load
Then haul
Then stage
Then rainy weather
Lost keys
Batteries
Blow-out at the side of the road
Strange way to start September

Home is dawn in a warm shower
Scrambled eggs on toast with butter
Another deep breath
Now something pure
Something sweet
Oh, this night is over!
A shot of Vodka and I'm off to sleep
Think I might need a few hours?

Doin' sound is doin' sound
Plug it in and it works
Right?
They'll dance and sing
Listen friend
You'd better pack politeness and patience
And tarps and doubles of *everything*
Sometimes it's a long, long night

First to arrive
Last to leave
F' ya bling
What's new in sound engineering?
Subtle nuances of stage lighting
A lifer is a lifer
Y' know what I mean

Doin' sound is doin' sound
All the roadrunning
Doin' sound is doin' sound
Can lead to bigger, better things

*You guys were, like … amazing!*

*And the sound…!*

# IT'S LIKE

It's like learning to pray on a rocket ship
Boosters fallin' away
It's like packing sand bags with your sneakers in
    the mud
Slip, slidin' away
It's like a room full of computers in a cave up in the
    hills
It's like standin' in front of Niagara Falls
After three days and nights of the darnedest
    cheap thrills
It's like a freshly fallen bed of silent snow
A warm sleeping bag
The cat stretching in the window

It's like a beloved actor
Who's taken his own life
What?
No...
How?
Why?
Run that by me twice
Turn on the radio
Pain is romantic
Death is exciting

Sugar, if you ain't a piece of chocolate cake
You is the lemon icing

It's like your pen running out of ink on a letter's
   last line
It's like running out of luck,
Knowing it would sometime
It's like only a particular brand of music will do
The best place to pick up women is at the
   supermarket
It's been documented in a movie or two

It's like a priestess
Big-eyed Olivia Newton John
Like a poster in a prison cell
Catwalk
Bikini
If y' get real close
Y' can see the sequined, softened folds of
   her femininity
She brought a choir to the temple of desire
I know Grandma 'd be so proud of me

It's like tumbleweeds or crystal balls
Heavenly bodies
Rolling stones

Oh, yes!

You will find new ways to pray!

Deeper than the ones you found formerly

Two English boys

Keith Richards always missed the Robert Johnson in
Brian Jones

It's like realizing you don't have to be stuck in a
pinball machine

It's like realizing that inside a pinball machine is the
only place you've ever been

It's like dealing with somebody who is clearly too
good for this world

There she goes

There she goes again

Back to where she came from

And you can't get right with her or without her

It's like a junkie in rehab on the phone in the hall

He thinks he's on to something no one else knows

There's a line here, man

Can you finish your call?

Oh, it's like…

It's like too damn much…

It's too revealing

She's tired and it's over
And the failure is as much my own…
You must produce a feeling

It's like a friend you can't keep
Who's always got something to prove
What does it mean to be "on the run?"
What is it to refuse to move?

It's like a barrel full of apples
Where one in the middle is rotten
It's like spitting out the window
When the window isn't open

It's like beets
When all there is is beets to eats
Wished I'd a' planted carrots
But all there is is beets
Beets
And more beets
Wished I'd a' planted green beans
Or turnips
But all there is is beets
Beets to eats
Beets
*Beets!*

## SAYING VESPA

And now for her next passive osmotic permutation:
Madonna will read a Patti Smith poem while dressed
in blue uniform, trying not to fall asleep working
at the Greyhound Bus Terminal reservation desk
in Poughkeepsie.

# HOW DOES IT FEEL?

How does it feel?

Feels like getting written off the page
Feels like someone got murdered
On New Year's Eve

Feels like strange things have happened
Like never before
Feels like your head just caught
The kitchen cabinet door

Feels like ice water in the veins
Feels like Abraham himself must've felt
When he heard Sarah's laughter in the
Desert's remains

It really is so sweet of you
To be so nice to me
Man, they can kill you with kindness
Face down in a field, tied up to a tree

How does it feel?

Feels like I'm sittin' at a table
With a long look on my face
Feels like somewhere in the deal his wounds
   would heal
No more bleedin' all over the place

Feels like what's known as "foot-in-mouth disease"
Neighbors raving on about huge conspiracies

Feels like a family reunion
Where everyone keeps going to the junk drawer
One's lookin' for toothpicks
Another, for a pin
And another for a sharp pair of scissors

It really is sweet of you to be so nice to me
What we hand each other
In this life
Our eternity

How does it feel?

Feels like the morning is lost
And the enemy has come ashore
Feels like anything is up for sale
First and foremost, entertainment's whore

You were once a stranger in this town
Maybe you can tell me
How it might feel?
Cacophony!
Feels like it would to you
If you stuck around here as long as me

I hope G-d isn't listening
But it feels like I'd rather be dead
Feels like another long rainy night
With all of it running in and out of my head

It really is sweet of you to be so nice to me
The 'jealous guy syndrome' hits so abruptly

How does it feel?

Could it be that a river caught on fire?
Is the smokestack sky an early grave?
Feels like every man's conscience
Is vile and depraved

Feels like a temple
A mosque, a church, a shrine
Donuts and coffee
I'll go get in line

Everybody wants to go to Heaven
But nobody wants to die
Everybody wants to love a woman
But no one wants to try it on for size

It really is sweet of you to be so nice to me
What's a far-fetched stretch to some
Is to others, normalcy

How does it feel?

Feels like knocking nails into a hardwood floor
With your forehead brow
Feels like the whole world's asleep
In a sleep so deep
' wouldn't want to wake 'em up now

Feels like the bottom's fallen out
Gotta make the most of standing in place
A woman's soul is a corkboard with tacks
A man's is just something that disintegrates

Feels like a broken mind
With no cure to fix it
Feels like gettin' into Heaven
An' findin' there's no TV set

It really is sweet of you to be so nice to me
Warheads for Co-Co Chanel
Truffles for Igor Stravinsky

How does it feel?

Feels like what'd be to be a boy scout in Vietnam
Feels like findin' out the hard way
That no one gives a damn[15]

Feels like a rainy day over clouded moats
The only thing left to do
Is to chant the keepers' quotes

Feels like deicide
As a child's dilemma
Fortune and fame
Neither is to be what they claim[16]
I hate to be the one t' have t' tell ya

It really is sweet of you to be so nice to me
Look, it's a blimp!
Where?
There
It's coming in for a landing

Feels like the vanishing act of imaginary friends
Feels like there's no way to stay and make amends
Feels like all your love's in vain
Dead poets, black swans, purple rain

Feels like the tantrum of a child
Sustained, harsh, and loud
Feels like inspiration
From impossibly scripted clouds

It really is so sweet of you to be so nice to me
Still got that same bad taste in my mouth
What I let go of
And how she went and laid down her money

How does it feel?

Feels like it's bad out there
Feels like a bird's nest in her hair
Feels like a cop meeting a quota
You'll be sorry some day
Don't say I never told ya

Feels like you're spinning your wheels
Repeating yourself

Yes, repeating yourself
Feels like the noose of poverty
The filthy rag of wealth

Feels like what he said to her
And what she said to him
Feels like finally leaving the docks
'Cause your ship won't be comin' in

It really is sweet of you to be so nice to me
What I've done
And have *not* done
In flowing down so free

# SONG FOR LISA MIMOSA

Lisa
You came to me at a time
When I'd been so recently peeled
You were so smart and so bright
You always left me healed

And I was stuck walking backwards
And you were like a sign
Leading me back to the day
To paths I could not find

Lisa
I needed you in a thousand ways
But my heart was like a snare
Life with you was life above the maze
You were a catch
And a catch is rare

And you had a way of saying things …
You were getting through to me
"Hey, I don't want to steal your dreams from
    you, baby"
"And what's goin' on … uh … that you can't see?"

I can see you comin' at me at the Savoy
"Woody's on the Beach"
You had your brown lenses in gold frames on
That was on New Year's Eve
The guitarist on stage …
We didn't even know it
Fifth Street at midnight with Ronnie's friend,
   Eric Clapton

Do you remember that shoreline
On a chilly Mediterranean night?
We couldn't get warm in an abandoned life boat
I remember we faced each other
But we couldn't make it right
A hopeless case is a case without hope, all right

Lisa
We're in the Old City
"You don't talk that way here"
Am I to apologize because you feel bad?
Beck went on about regulating
And Steve Miller was like Elvis
Parking lot
Chicken soup
Westphalia flag

Georgia Nights
Alaska's lights
A shooting star
A plane ride home
Twin Peaks Boulevard
Fog in the lights
The last bit of hash in the bag
Your Tibetan book of Om

Lisa
Ain't life but a series of prematurely made decisions?
Wanna know something?
Don't eat bruised persimmons
Too bad
So sad
Bygones
*Bygones*
Sometimes I use your attitude to get a rise out
    of people
You're always in here somewhere for me to rely on

Lisa
Ain't it strange that we don't exist to him
As a joint of anything at all…?
I love it that you keep that shot of Tom Waits

By the stairway in the hall
I'm going to get my coat
I feel the breath of a storm
Two strands of time, neatly tied

So long again, Lisa Mimosa
In the French inhaler, she calls him Norm

# JAPANESE

Would I move to Japan?
It's a green land
I'm sure they've got a few women as ugly as I am
Japan
Maybe I never been a true, red-blooded American
To think I'd just get up one day and move to Japan...
I'd learn the letters of their alphabet on LSD
Retrain my throat and learn to speak the way
   they speak
My tutors would all be English majors from
   Beacon Hill
Double-majoring in physics
And they'd all have *tits*
How hard we'd work on proper diction and accents
One's at the door right now!

Maybe in the next life
I'll be a good lookin' Japanese kid
Listenin' to Van Halen's first two albums
A Pamela Anderson poster on my bedroom wall
I'll be m-a-s-t-e-r-b-a-t-i-n'!
*Son?*

Japan
Baseball stadiums
Big dreams
They probably know "Take Me Out to the
    Ball Game"
(And I heard they dig Thelonious Monk, too)
They probably eat hot dogs
Coca Cola
Kirin Beer
It's not so far away as it seems

Japan
Garth Brooks sells out there
He's lionized
Ask him!
Japan
Live at Budokan
Cheap Trick
Neil Diamond
Heart
Even Bobe Dee-laan

Japan
They've got unleaded fuel
Those good cars they make

Y' run 'em and y' run 'em and they never break
You can build three Hondas out of a single Cadillac
They got go-kart handling, man
Japan
They've got funny eyes
They talk strange
Godzilla!
Japan
Green tea
Bamboo
Raw fish and rice
"They call it 'sushi' or something."

To the Japanese
Their fine China is like our paper plates and
   plastic dishes
Really!
Funny, they call it "China!"
And I love their big, beautiful, bounteous faces
So pretty…

And the food, yes
They don't get obese
Full of heart disease
Bonsai

Hari-Kari
Samurai
More wasabi, please

In the next life
I might be in love
With Connie Chung's grandchildren
I wonder if I'll mess everything up again
I'm probably bound to find religion
Connie…

Now to find me that Ivy League
English-speaking
Extravagantly radiant
Concert pianist-type Japanese woman…
*Tits…*

# DAVE'S SONG

I once knew a man
Who knew his way around a recording studio
   rather handily
The control room was his second home
His pallet
His professionalism, his professionality
His name was Dave, Dave Reuter
He was one who gathered momentum in life
Yes, siree
He was reserved
But you could tell right away that he was not ordinary

I had sore fingertips
He was a hard man of strings
He helped me get down some spirited recordings
He put an early seventies Marshall amp
In a hallway of Mexican tile
Tina Turner's brazier stood in front of a microphone
He didn't get along with the engineer
It got a little sticky in there for a while

We had a baby grand piano
And another guitar
And drums on the floor

We tuned our instruments
To his antique, black and white strobe tuner
Seanmon didn't like Dave too much
Seanmon can be distracted as such
Joel and Lee and Horach and me
We were eighteen
Recording live
A group
A young bunch
*What a rush!*

Somehow this dude, Dave
Early in his life
Wound up at The Record Plant in Los Angeles
All through the seventies
He knew The Wrecking Crew
They came in to record over
What the young groups were only attempting

Dave knew the legendary record man, Bob Johnson
Dave and Bob were both hardy Texans
He described a few sessions
Engineering for none other than Bob Dylan
Before "Desire" or "Blood on the Tracks"
"He told me Bob seemed like he'd rather have been
    somewhere else"

I was over at Dave's house a few times
It wasn't fancy but he kept it neat
He lived with a woman then
Lauren
They seemed happy
She was studying voice at the university

He had a drafting table next to his desk
He could draw anything you asked him to
He once asked me which comics in the funnies
   I liked best
When I said "Sally Forth", he said "No, 'Calvin
   and Hobbes'"
Looked at me like, "Man, what's up with you?"

He drove a silver Volkswagen Dasher
That he said, "could not be killed"
He kept a cream colored Fender Strat upside down in
   his closet
And a J-45 Gibson Hummingbird
He told me about Jimmy Rogers in Nashville

Dave'd kick back on his couch
Spark up a joint 'n' watch the evening news
Once I called him to tell him Salvador Dali was
   going to be on 60 Minutes

He called me an angel
His voice changed
He said, "Thank you, man. Thank you!"


He had been a photographer in the Air Force
   years before
He'd seen things that haunt and scar a soul
I asked him about LSD one time
He said, "Life is about diamonds and shit
And LSD is the confirmation of it
"Kid, isn't it about time for you to go home?"


He was efficient in his kitchen
He cut up a steak on a wooden block
I picked up a jar of Jamaican bird peppers
He and Lauren said
*"No!*
*Don't!*
*Stop!*
People have been known to go into shock!
Jamaican bird peppers
Wash your hands
One touch
Bloodshot
You can't fucking imagine how hot"

In Miami
In Coconut Grove
Somewhere down the line…
Dave built studios with detail and excellence
People there with long hair
Who needed a ramp or a fence
Bar rooms
Storefronts
Pool decks
Ramps
Stairways and driveways
He made a living by completing projects

No one in the neighborhood knows what's become
   of him
None of his neighbors
None of his friends
He was a solo flyer
That much was true of him
He knew all of Aldous Huxley's Messianism
He asked me whether I thought art imitated life
Or life imitated art
I must've responded in a vague kind of way
But the question stuck with me
And that is what he no doubt wished to impart

I'm just thinkin' of someone
Who put a shakin' on my life some years ago
He was serious in a way
That said something about the outside world you
    didn't know
He was just a guy out there
Too talented and too real
Didn't get any big breaks
He knew every riff off of the Stones' album
    *Steel Wheels*
This cat was a walking earthquake

And one more thing about this Dave Reuter
Some kind of South Florida friend
He could sing three part harmonies with REO
    Speedwagon or Van Halen
He'd played with Nils Lofgren in Topanga Canyon
When Topanga Canyon had no boundaries
Once he said I should consider him the enemy
He said that he thought the rich were stupid, mostly
What was relevant to him?
What was relative to him?
He was just holdin' on, wasn't he

I'm glad to write this song
A toast to a music man who gave it a ride

The audio arts
Where people don't just mull around
With chicken on a stick and a coat and tie
And to the great state of Texas
Where they raise 'em with promise and pride
"Harvest the nobility of others," he told me
*Harvest nobility...*
Wouldn't that put God on your side?


So then
Another round!
To Dave
Dave Reuter
Wherever you are
A scoundrel of the highest order!
Genius!
Madman!
Rock 'n' roller!
Take you to the leader of the band at the border

# LAUNDRIES, BARS, HAMBURGERS, BOOKSTORES

It's 4:00 in the morning
Can ya get a decent cup of coffee in this dipshit town?

Hey man, How ya doin'?
Mind if I sit down?
Where am I from?
Well, I'm from Miami town
Where none of the women ever had fathers
And the men all bathe in Paco Rabanne
I've come north
Alone
In search of the perfect ice cream cone

Where do I stay?
I rented a little place down the road
It's sixty yards off the beach
All these buses are full of meth monsters
I come 'n' go amongst skivvy, lost redneck creeps
My place is no bigger than a post office box
I had the landlord change the locks

Quite a crowd…
There's bikers and soldiers
There's a blues club
Skateboarders
All night there's sweet weed in the air
Side-pipes loud
I look out from my balcony
Yeah
Tank-tops 'n' titties
Quite a crowd

I've got a banjo and some drums
I write
That makes me a writer
A writer I am
I even memorize some of my work and sing it
There's an open mic night at the café out on
    the strand

I've heard that livin' alone makes ya crazy
I've got my dogs
Somewhere there's a woman who's right for me
My comfort zone
She's wearing leather sandals or clogs
She's got a sense of humor all her own

I left my wife in my first year of marriage
Came here and slept behind a dumpster in a
   parking lot
Which is now a Pizza Hut
Worked out of a labor pool
Gave blood
In this same freakin' town
In this same freakin' neighborhood

I've got a son
He's sixteen years old
His name is Levi, bless him
Looks just like his mama
He loves Pink Floyd and Tom Waits and Jerry Garcia
Makes good grades
He's prettier than I ever was or ever will be
Lives in a small town with his brothers
Just east of the Everglades

I got a sister lives in California
Divorced a hedge fund broker
Now she owns half of Japan
She's a swinger
Dating a singer
Her name, by the way, is Jan

"Why don't you get a job, my dear brother?
How much this time, little Machie man?"

I'm thinking maybe my kid 'll come
For a few weeks next summer
But it's not likely to happen
My ex-wife, she's pretty as a flower
Mean as a snake
As you might imagine

I didn't know this diner even existed
This whole place is one major strip mall
You can get a decent bagel by the water tower
A bunch of Jewish gals sayin', "Ya'll"
Each one been married forever

Y' seen that guy in front of the carwash
Dancin' around with that blue and white sign?
That's me, motherfucker!
Yeah, I tell people I'm in advertising

I've counted eight surf shops between here and the
    army base
And four churches
Big aren't they?

I was walkin' by
And I just stood there with my headphones on
Staring at the stained glass
Girls in their summer clothes drivin' by
Sunroof
T-tops
Each one crazier than the last

I don't get high much any more
'Cept for a little weed through the daylight hours
But when I first got here
At the Salt Air Motel
There were these two ladies with that yellowish white
    protein powder

More blue jeans than I could handle
Quite a scene
I could hardly believe what was happening to me!
Giggles at my door
Like cheerleaders
Miss Peters!
If one wasn't twenty-eight, the other wasn't
    thirty-four
Like bein' in a Willie Nelson tune
Steak 'n' eggs couldn't happen too soon

I turned on the TV
There was more blood and guts in four hours
Than a veteran of war ever seen
And then
There was a movie trailer
About the world comin' to an end
Worse than a bad dream
I turned it off sayin' I'd never turn one on again

The weather girl had on a mini-skirt and bra
It was half past 7:00 a.m.
I'd just come from 'glitzy' Miami
Tits and ass everywhere
It's pretty much the same
Even at 7:00 a.m

And mister
Sometimes I get so tired of thinking
Of all the places I don't want to go
And all the things I *don't* want to do
I *don't* want to go to India
I've never been
I *don't* want to join the gym
I'd rather walk to the ocean and wade on in
I *don't* want a good job on Wall Street
I *don't* want to get herpes or heart disease

I'm not into the likes of Travis Tritt much
The Opera
The Circus
A New car
New tires
Pizza
Pepsi
Rap music
Starsky and Hutch

I like to make soup
Like my mother does
Beet and carrot smoothies, cuz!
Club sandwiches
Praline ice cream
Georgia peaches
I like navel oranges in the sun
Fortune cookies
Iced lychees
Hard pears
Stinky cheese
Airport Cinnabons (Oh…)
I love cigarettes
And I'll smoke 'em 'til I'm *dead*
Yes, I roll my own
And I vape … therefore I am

A cup of coffee 2,000 miles from home
The sight of people holding hands
Who somehow still seem glad to be wed
Fast boats
Faster women
Elephants
Manatees
Whales
Dolphins
British Colombian Hippies
I like mushroom tea outside a museum with a
   handsome gal
Japanese motorcycles crashin' into one another
Goin' fast as hell

Mister, I'll tell ya who I listen to...
I listen to the softer side of rock in Jackson Browne
And those songs by Petty, Springsteen, and Dylan
Marc Knopfler, Sinead O'Conner, U2, and the
   Clash
The Black Crows' Chris Robinson
I like and I listen
And I listen again
Like I liked and I listened to it all back then
*Dude, will you pass me the half-and-half?*

Looks like rain
The sun 'll be up soon
It's the weekend
Rain or shine I'm on the sands
I'm in the dunes
I've got a killer wetsuit
Had it custom cut a few years back
Still fits like a glove to the hand
The naval base is north
Cape Canaveral's down south
Happy dogs with tennis balls in their mouths

Starbucks makes a pretty good cup
But that place by the bridge got the three-egg
  mushroom omelet
So…
For my dog, a cat
For my cat, a bird
For my bird, a fish
For my fish, a worm
I'm reading a book about being *Bright Sided*
*Nickeled and Dimed*
*Baited and Switched*
Barbara Ehrenreich takes it to term
Every stitch

Right, well … dude
Thank you for listening to me ramble
I guess I been kinda ramblin' and ramblin' on
I musta needed someone to talk to…
And I didn't catch your name, friend…
Yeah…?
Kim?
You're folks fucking named you Kim?
Are you puttin' me on?
Wait…
I … I've heard of that before
I guess it's kinda cool
Kim…
Kim is better than Mark or Fred or Tim
Oh to have been been named Tim…


Dude, I've got to make the most of my time here
I'm gonna grow my hair down to my feet,
   so strange
I'm gonna look like a walking, talking
   mountain range
I'm gonna go to the golf course carryin' a
   New York Times
Shoot a few holes
Blow their minds

Then maybe I'll ride to Omaha on a horse
And do the same thing at another blessed
   golf course[17]
Whip out my B-flat harmonica at 2:00 a.m.
   and blow
Get into myself
Piss in the wind
Put on a lil show
See ya round, dude…
Kim

# TITTY TIME BAR SONG

Iddy biddy squiddy titty
Bubble butt galore
All I call mine
You can call yours

It isn't such a crime
It isn't such a sin
Larry ... Hey, this is Lisa
Leslie, that's Tim

Iddy biddy squiddy titty
Funky underpants
Wanna lambada, baby?
Tango, fandango
So you think you can dance!

No, it isn't such a crime
It isn't such a sin
The fire inside
Trade your sneer for a grin

Hey bartender, say what ...
Say what!

This round's on me
We can all go back to my place,
Here, throw me your keys

Iddy biddy squiddy titty
Ecstasy, microdots
I'm getting the chills
Mercy me, baby
Gimme all you gots

The microphone smells like a beer
The old harmonica hums
Loud, loud guitars
Fat strappin' drums

I've got my last clean shirt on
It smells of stale perfume
I've come two hundred miles
Only to be here in this barroom

Iddy biddy squiddy titty
Spin her all around
Give the girl a kiss
Get into the sound

You and your honey babe
Go to a blues club in town
You come here for to rock and roll
To get hit
To get down

The Lounge Lizards
Titty time
Frank' s trio
Titty time
The Allman Brothers
Titty time
Ry Cooder
Titty time
T-Bone Burnett
Titty time
Lone Justice with Steve Van Zandt
Titty time
Jam Sandwich
Titty time
Gatemouth Brown
Titty Time
Little Feat
Titty time

Paris, Texas
Titty time
Marhsa Ball
Titty time!
It's closin' time...
Last call!
Titty time!

*Hey, baby*

# HOUSE OF THE RISING SUN
## (ALTERNATE LYRICS)

There is a house in New Orleans
They call the rising sun
And it's been the ruin of many a poor boy
And me, I know I'm one

My mother was a tailor
She sewed my new blue jeans
Daddy was a bank robber
The spawn of New Orleans

The only thing a gambler needs
Is a suitcase and a trunk
The only time he's satisfied
Is when he's good and drunk

Tell my baby sister
Not to do what I have done
Don't spend your life in sin and misery
In the house of the rising sun

I've got one foot on the platform
The other foot on the train
No one tells you the day you're born
It's the same; it's all the same

There is a house in New Orleans
They call the rising sun
Welcome to the land of the living dead
On the lam; you're on the run

The lazy river's rolling
The church's bell is rung
Children, don't you go down there, no
It don't mean no good t' no one

A man should never be
Where a man he don't belong
It don't mean no good to no one to be
In the house of the rising sun

There is a house in New Orleans
They call the rising sun
And it's been the ruin of many a poor boy
And me, I know I'm one

# LAUGH A LITTLE

If you don't learn to laugh a little
You will one day be so weakened
As to drive the blade in
If you don't learn to laugh a little
You'll keep comin' back to the same old thing
You'll put your fool head on the tracks
And won't pull it loose
If you don't learn to laugh a little …
Where would we be without Dr. Seuss?

The tryin' man
The cryin' man
One day he'll come to say
"How could all this be happening to me?"
Poverty is demoralizing…
*Poverty*
Shuffled are the virtues of purity
Isn't it a pity?

*Let me hear y' sing…!*
*"Train to Jordan"*
*"You Got to Walk That Lonesome Valley"*
*"Jesus is Real to Me"*

"*Dial Him Up and tell Him What You Want*"
*Choir, sing!*


If you don't learn to laugh a little
You could crash your car at the age of twenty-seven
If you don't learn to laugh a little
They'll ask you *why* when you get to heaven
Don't you laugh…?
Even a little?
Laugh a little
A spark of hilarity
Personality
The church lifted its ban on it in 1623
I look at you; I smile … you *monkey*
If you don't learn to laugh a little
You'll take more than a second at happy hour
We all love to laugh
No matter how forced it may be


*Tonight!*
*Ladies drink free*
*Wednesdays, Thursdays … Fridays*


Come on! Fancy a pint? Join me
Barkeep, make that a double
It's a cold one out there, *oo-weee*

Let's get that first kiss outta the way right now,
   you and me
Bottom's up, everybody!
To learn to laugh a little, eh?
Fifty years from now you'll get
Psilocybin mushrooms on your paté
At the ol' McCafé

How do I learn to laugh a little, Padre?
Getting your lessons learned isn't always so funny
To laugh, Buddha caught a fish
Loves his spicy dish
Crossin' things off a bucket list
Wearing your ugliest sweater the whole week of
   Christmas
Call now and you can own these completely restored
   and remastered
Episodes of *Laugh-in* on CBS

Don Rickles with Johnny Carson
Flip Wilson, Goldie Hawn
In a highchair feeding sweet Lilly Tomlin
John Cleese
Richard Pryor, Steven Wright
Seinfeld, Shandling
David Letterman

He gets his own line
And we say his name twice…
David Letterman
George Carlin
Don White
Andy Kauffman

*Take a piss!*
*Take a piss!*
*You might be a redneck*
*If you hold your fork like this*

Billy Preston on the organ
The piano and the electric bass
Billy 'd stand right there
Love to sing to you
Bring a smile to your face
A tryin' man on the organ
A cryin' man
That's Billy Preston
Can't help but sing
Listenin' to him
They called him "The fifth Beatle," man
Or was that Eric Claption?
George Martin
How do you learn to laugh?

Remember that you were once a child
A jumpy little kid
Wanting only to get *wild*
Laughter
Y' gonna need a little to live
Laughter
They say the best you can do is forgive

*Hey…!*
*Snap out of it*
*Just forget about it*
*A little smile*
*Gimme some sugar*
*And a little laughter*

# RAGS

Pick that rag up off the floor
There's a lot of things you can use a rag for
To clean up a mess
Formica
Marble
Ceramic
Wood
Glass
Scrub a stain
Dust a shelf
A rag is a shred of something else

Use a rag as the tail of a kite
Stuff a rag up your neighbor's tailpipe
You can use a rag in a quilt
Tie a whole bunch together
You always got more than enough underneath the
   kitchen sink
That's where they gather

Use a rag to wipe the sweat from your brow
If it gets too wet just squeeze it out
Tie a rag to the end of a stick

If y' got somethin' to carry that's a good way t'
    carry it
A rag's a good thing to have in the glove
    compartment of your car
Pinch the dipstick, the oil indicator

A rag 'll clean the corners of your room
Or grab those dust bunnies under the couch
Spring cleanin's in April, not June
Don't you rattail me…
*Ouch!*
*Yer dead!*

Are you on the rag?
Are you thick?
I've told you twice I don't like that expression …
    dear!

A rag can be raised to declare surrender
A rag?
A flag
Sew some rags together
Make a sail
You can sail away from here
Sew some rags together

Make a pad for a chair
You can sit down right here
Wanna beer?
Wrap a rag around a handle
Dipped in oil, you get a torch
Gets those damned mosquitos off your porch!
A rag's a gauze in a first aid kit
Hope I never have to tie a tourniquet
Rags for your bicycle chain
The sprocket
The bell
The grips
Start with the seat
Neat!

Rags work fine for everyday spills
Skip paper towels in your budget or bills
They're made of cotton
So there aren't any trees cut down and killed

A rag to clean your guitar strings
A rag for drum shells and drum skins
A rag shines cymbals
A clean cymbal *rings*
And shines

And splashes
And rides
*Yeaaahhhhh ...Go!*


Ragtop
Ragtime
Ragtag
Raggedy Anne and Raggedy Andy
Ragweed
Do rag
Snotrag
Raggamuffin
*Who writes for this rag?*


*I asked you to pick that rag up off the floor, please*


Rags sure come in handy
Don't they...?

# KID GONE BAD

What d'ya think?

I ain't got the blues enough to sing?

Am I supposed t' get mad?

Die harder?

Cough up a bigger ring?

Y' must be aware that some of this would hit
     another person

As punishing

You must be a Scorpio

But who knows what house?

Does any of this have any binding?

I sang "The Rose" in the heart of Miami

I'd say half the people stopped their chatting
     and drinking

Yvette Carrion was in the crowd

She checked the key

Put her palm to her ear

And chimed in for the third verse

I blew her a kiss

Just as the song was ending

It was late in the evening

Robert Plant showed up sick with a sore throat

Had a temperature

David Bricker performed a Django Reinhardt
  overture
Industrial-sized telephone cable spools
Made for hip furniture

How this one likes to fly
Lies on her belly like a big fish
"Nurse, Send in Coco's boy!"
Nobody's home
She likes that in a guy
If they could get close enough
They'd murder God
(Birthrights)
Dust talk in your room back in the war
To be the first family
Of all she's endorsed
And all she's left in command
The carpaccio you'd have to perpetually make
Of your free hand
She waited for me like I waited for her
This wouldn't be what the worst is
If this wasn't what the worst is
You can feel a living death
Deep in the night
Under the bed

In the closet

Over in the corner

I'm a lion

I'm a tiger

Y' know what?

After dealin' in this game

Y' got to make the queen disappear

*Consigliére*

*Monsignor*

How on earth are these people ever to celebrate one
another?

Sweet Jesus!

# MAYBE FRENCH?

Maybe I was a Frenchman in the last life
Always dreaming of the finest things
Finding my feet underneath me
Flutes and drums and strings
Mediaeval things
Calvinists and guillotines

Dreams of wines of legend ...
Wines of legend
Vintages rumored
Wines from tables where kings and queens dined
In centuries the former

French doors
Black wood corridors
Barrels in rows
Galleries
Time and temperatures

Always dreaming
Of things you can't have
Is it not a French thing
To be somewhat disenchanted?

We French, how do you say it…?
We live to know how sweet life can be
We only have two ways or modes or speeds:
Dire misery
Or
Isn't this event supposed to be celebratory!?

I know some French
I know the word *suave*
Maybe we could *rendezvous*
*Café au lait* at the Louvre?
*Au revoir*

You make me laugh
That's what I guess I didn't get enough of from
  you, Michelle
I remember you oh so well, Michelle
I do
Yes, I do

A young child
In the yard of a house in the country
His palms to the spokes of a bike wheel
Slowly spinning
Grandpa, can we please go for a ride?

Finish your lunch child
Grandpa's peddling

From youth I was told
Of fine chalices at meals
With ballroom dancing
And silly nursery rhymes
And wines so fine
The very thought of them intoxicating the mind

I must have heard the word from my uncles
My uncles sang songs about smashing brothels
Laughing, they would rise from the table
And be on their way
Surely, much to my mother's dismay

Look Michelle
How the young drifter walks, stick and bag
Michelle, shouldn't we invite him for cheese and
     bread?
I'm not going to argue with you, Michelle
Not over passing company
And you're not going to hear me say, "please"
He can sleep in the loft
Do chores in the morning

Oh, Michelle
How you can be so *stoopeed* and boring!?

To be French
What does it mean?
Passion rules the arrow flying
700 years is what Paris is
Pipes and electricity
Wires frayed and frying
Every summer we climb the Pyrenees
Whole town's in yellow jerseys
*Baguette? Brie? Perrier?*
Yes, please, *s'il vous plaît*

Paper said some vintage magic was just auctioned
   off
Lock and key
Sotheby's
Gloved hands presenting the stuff
It went to one Count Olaf for an undisclosed
   amount

Is it that I am so unfulfilled
That these feelings rule my heart?
Ruled by some absence
French madness

Flummoxed
Flabbergasted
Always off the chart

A thousand cups of coffee on the Boulevard
What did people smoke before tobacco?
The face on him, Depardeau, Gerard
The mayor of Nice is a rock star named Bono

One day I'll have a pot to piss in
That I can call my own
Till then the storefront display reads
*Adidas, Renault, Esprit, Citröen*

What do I do more
Spend my time craving the things I'll never know of?
Or do I mull around, scuffling my feet?
The world doesn't know Charles Aznavour
He grew up here
A mime
A clown
A ballad in a bar
A singer on the street
Aznavour
The man
*C'est Magnifique!*

I would rather be a cat in the jungle

Jaguar

Panther

Tiger

Leopard

The French…

They eke out a living

Struggle for a bundle

Riots in the streets

Reasons we've heard


I could use a half-carafe

Half a carafe of Sauvignon

If you insist, I will taste the Boujolais Nouveau

*La plata fromage*

French women don't get fat

Now I will try to make my way home

# THESE CHILDREN

Did these children find it in their hearts
To forgive one another their quarreling?
Did they keep for one another
Enough respect for love to spring?
Did they maintain the kind of truths
That kept a holiness their own?
Were there gatherings to prove a house a home?
Did they help each other like only family can?
Could they bury the hatchet?
Did they seek out and gather any amongst them
   who ran?
Did they include themselves in each other's plans?
Did they place blessed children in each others' arms?
Were there tears of joy?
A clasping of hands?

Was there mutual admiration?
Were Yahrzeit candles lit?
Did they gain wisdom?
A healthy sense of caution?
Bravery…
Was there patience?
Did they covet the trait of patience?
Loving kindness?

Well wishes?
Modesty?
Fairness?
Judiciousness?
What was the essence?
Did they honor their peace?

What of ambition?
The full breadth of their freedom
Personal bests
Worldliness
What was it of them their mother held dearest?
Did they see their father as one who cherished
    their innocence?
Preserved their childishness?
Their youthfulness?
What was encouraged?
Discouraged?
Fitting and never-too-harsh punishments

Did they dream of their ancestors far beyond?
Did all that counts add up to such connection?
Did they live for things in life worthwhile?
Did they play music on drums and strings?
What was the dance they found themselves
    dancing?

What were their hopes and dreams?
Did some of them excel and rise to the heights of
  learning?


Hope they don't get mixed up
With any heartless, know-nothing, star-struck,
  fame-strapped opportunists —
Tyrannical types you see out there these days
Runnin' around town
Well dressed
In expensive automobiles
Phones to their ears...
With their children

# LAST DECEMBER LATE

Last December late
I had a party with Mr. Happy, my mate
We ate ginger snaps and chocolate cherry ice cream
There was rum on the counter
And this disappearing powder
Naked people on the TV screen
Took me days to get back
My mind was dislodged
Outta whack
Pots in a sack
Dislodged
Hodge-podged
Put upon
By angels who, for a night, became demons
Ever since I seen that girl with the white pants on
That girl with the white pants on …
What'd you do for New Year's?
Did my laundry
No, what did you *do* for New Year's?
My resolution was to play along wherever life may
    find me
And hide this cable bill…
Bethany 'll have my hiney!

# PICTURES OF PETTY

I was reading poetry in New Orleans, in August, early September of 2017, a week after Tom Petty died. I'd packed all my favorite pictures of him and set out to Xerox them for keepsakes, and to make a few montages to post around town. And I did just that—on Oak Street, Magazine, St. Charles, and Canal.

In every place, as I squatted down to cover the blank sides of the pages with epoxy, the people passing by stopped and cooed, "Oh, Tom," or just "Petty." It was kind. It was sad. It was beautiful. It was empty.

On Royal Street, I found a space for a mural and as I shook the can of glue, someone came up to me. "I own this building. Just what do you think you're doing?"

I looked him right in the eye. "I'm memorializing Tom Petty," I explained.

He paused for second. "Because it's for Tom, I'll let it go."

That's the thing about losing him, and what it'll be like as our much-loved companions ascend. We want to do something to help us remember. We want them back for a moment—that *something*. We want to say goodbye. We want another encore.

# AUTHOR'S NOTE

This may be a little unorthodox, but as I've just gone on about "big moments" I've had in my own high-fidelity rock 'n' roll fandom, I'd like to recognize and acknowledge a piano man — Arlan Feiles — who lived down this way for a while back in the late eighties. One of the truly accomplished and talented among us, he led the group, Natural Causes.

They lit it up at a backyard party one night last summer. Made me sing like a skinny black chick in church (All respect to skinny black chicks in church). I didn't know every last little thing about what he was puttin' down, but it was challenging of spirit and we were floored... *Floored!*

# ENDNOTES

1. Little Richard

2. Beach Boys

3. The Chiffons, "Chains"

4. Joe Walsh, "In The City"

5. Gershwin, George, "I Got Rhythm"

6. Dylan, Bob, "Highway 61 Revisited"

7. Springsteen, Bruce, "Born in the USA"

8. Pink, "Get the Party Started"

9. Dylan, Bob, "Gonna Change My Way of Thinkin"

10. Chumbawamba, "Tubthumping"

11. Tosh, Peter, "I've Learned Some Lessons in My Life"

12. Zevon, Warren, "Worrier King"

13. Zevon, Warren, "The Envoy"

14. Petty, Tom. "Nothin' to Me"

15. Traveling Wilburies, "Tweeter and the Monkey Man"

16. Dylan, Bob, "Just Like Tom Thumb's Blues"

17. Dylan, Bob, "I Shall Be Free"